# CONTENT STRATEGY
## for the Web

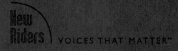

New Riders | VOICES THAT MATTER™

## Kristina Halvorson

# Content Strategy for the Web

**Kristina Halvorson**

New Riders
1249 Eighth Street
Berkeley, CA 94710
510/524-2178
510/524-2221 (fax)

Find us on the Web at: www.newriders.com
Visit www.contentstrategy.com for more information and to join the conversation.
To report errors, please send a note to errata@peachpit.com
New Riders is an imprint of Peachpit, a division of Pearson Education
Copyright © 2010 by Kristina Halvorson

Project Editor: Michael J. Nolan
Development Editor: Margaret S. Anderson, Stellarvisions
Production Editor: Tracey Croom
Copyeditor: Darren Meiss
Proofreader: Rose Weisburd
Indexer: James Minken
Cover designer: Aren Howell
Interior design and composition: Kim Scott, Bumpy Design

ISBN 13: 978-0-321-62006-4
ISBN 10:     0-321-62006-2

9 8 7 6 5 4 3

Printed and bound in the United States of America

*For the staff at Brain Traffic,*
*whose hard work, brave insights, and shared sense*
*of humor inspired every page that follows.*


*And for my husband John,*
*whose loving patience and support made this book possible.*

## ACKNOWLEDGMENTS

I don't care who you are: If you're writing a book, you're asking dozens of people for some kind of assistance or support. And, if you're lucky, those people are as extraordinarily thoughtful, intelligent, responsive, and generous as the following individuals were during my work on this book.

My deepest thanks to…

**Melissa Rach,** who stepped in at the last minute to serve as technical editor. Melissa is responsible for creating much of the methodology discussed in Chapters 4, 5, and 6. She's an extraordinary content strategist and one of the smartest people I know; I can't give her enough thanks or credit for her amazing work. I'm lucky to have her as a colleague and friend.

**Peter Merholz,** who bravely invited me to Adaptive Path's offices in May 2008 to speak publicly for the first time about content strategy, and has since become a terrific mentor and friend.

**Jeffrey Zeldman,** both for encouraging my first *A List Apart* article, and for inviting me to take the stage at An Event Apart in 2009. There never was a better cheerleader.

**Rachel Lovinger, Jeffrey MacIntyre, Karen McGrane, Elena Melendy,** and **Ian Alexander,** my East Coast partners in content strategy crime. Big brains, big laughs. My favorite combination.

**Erika Hall,** the original Queen of Content, who taught me to love "e-mail" (not "email"), SNL shorts, and absinthe.

**Liz Danzico, Ginny Redish, Lou Rosenfeld, Dan Saffer,** and **Molly Wright Steenson,** who offered up intelligent insights, wonderful support, and their own personal networks to help bring this book to life.

**Carolyn Wood** and **Krista Stevens,** who both played important roles in the publication in "The Discipline of Content Strategy" in *A List Apart* Issue 274 in December 2008. Sections of this essay appear throughout this book.

**Clare O'Brien, Anne Caborn, Bob Doyle, Kevin Cornell,** and **Jesse James Garrett,** for granting the rights to use their illustrations and graphics in this book.

**Sean Tubridy**, for his magical illustration powers and mastery of Photoshop.

**Rahel Bailie, Bob Boiko, Sarah Bowen, Liz Danzico, Paul Ford, Colleen Jones, James Mathewson, Mark McCormick, Karen McGrane, Chris Moritz, Joe Pulizzi, Richard Sheffield,** and **Lisa Welchman,** for answering my questionnaires and granting such helpful interviews. Thanks for your input, insights, and general awesomeness.

**Margot Bloomstein, Jennifer Bohmbach, Amber Simmons, Craig Bromberg, Jennifer Bove, Jonathan Kahn, Erin Malone, Clare O'Brien,** and **Daniel Souza,** all of whom took the time to read and comment on early drafts of my toughest chapters.

**The participants in the 2009 IA Summit Content Strategy Consortium** and **the members of the Content Strategy Google Group.** Good work, you crazy trailblazers.

**Nancy Aldrich-Ruenzel and Michael Nolan,** who opened the door for this book to be published. Thank you for your shared vision, and for trusting me with this important subject. Also to **Margaret Anderson,** my development editor, and the entire team at New Riders.

**Erin Anderson, Christine Benson, David Bowen, Meghan Casey, Katie Dohman, Josh Foldy, Angie Halama, Beth Johnson, Angie King, Melissa Rach, Elizabeth Saloka, Julie Vollenweider,** and **Amy Wallace**. There are many things I'm not very good at. But I am apparently brilliant at hiring smart-as-hell, resourceful, committed, deeply good people. Thanks for your hard work, research assistance, and terrific insights. And, of course, for putting up with me on a daily basis.

**Paul and Jackie Halvorson,** my parents, for their enthusiasm about and support for my work.

**And, most of all, my family.** As any writer knows, it's impossible to write a book without the steadfast support of loved ones. My two young children have been as patient as possible with Mama-writing-the-book, stopping by my desk several times a day for kisses and hugs. And my amazing husband John took over most of our shared responsibilities while I worked, offering me unlimited support and encouragement. Thank you. I love you.

# CONTENTS

## CREATE

## GOVERN

# BEFORE WE BEGIN…

· · · · · · · · · · · · · · · · · · · · · · · · · · · · · · · ·

WELL, HELLO THERE.

Thanks for picking up this book. I like you already.

At the risk of sounding presumptuous, I'm going to go ahead and assume you're interested in fixing your web content. Or helping someone else fix theirs. And that's terrific. It's why I wrote this book.

But first, I need to clarify a few things about what this book is and what it is not. Bear with me. It's what we authors do.

## WHAT THIS BOOK IS

**This book is an introduction to the emerging practice of content strategy.** It provides a high-level overview of the benefits, roles, activities, and deliverables associated with content strategy.

I wrote this book for companies, agencies, and beginning practitioners who want to understand what content strategy is, why it's important, and how to go about getting it done.

This book also makes the case for content strategy as a legitimate, necessary practice in the web consulting, design, and development industries.

Finally, this book describes processes and methodologies that may be applied to all kinds of content: text, images, video, and audio. However, most often I talk about content as text, and here's why:

- **Text is everywhere.** Today, most of the content on the web is text. We search for it in articles, blog posts, product descriptions, reviews, and more. We depend on it to tell us which video we're about to watch, or where to click in order to complete our purchase. We create it ourselves using social media channels, blogs, wikis, and more. Text instructs, guides, informs, confirms, communicates, connects.

- **Text is different.** Video, audio, and images have established, familiar production processes that have been around for decades. Yes, when we deliver these assets online, they require a different kind of preparation from when we deliver them elsewhere. But typically, once these assets are online, we don't worry about them again until it's time to move them or remove them. They don't require the same care and feeding as text.

- **Text is messy as hell.** As anyone who's ever dealt with web content knows, text is a moving target with multiple owners and stakeholders. It's the most complex kind of content to produce, and it's the easiest to lose control of. (I talk a lot about why this is and how to fix it in this book, so I'll stop myself from going on my usual rant. That comes later.)

## WHAT THIS BOOK IS NOT

**This book is not The Complete Guide to Everything You Ever Need to Know About Content Strategy, Ever.** Frankly, I'm not sure if that book can be written yet. A lot about content strategy is still being figured out. The good news is that, at the time of this writing, there are a lot of really smart people talking about it—on blogs, in forums, on Twitter, in conversations and conferences. Processes and deliverables are evolving and being shared in the larger community. All good things.

At any rate, here are a few specific topics this book intentionally does not cover (at all, or in detail):

- Content management systems (CMS) strategy (software selection, design, and implementation).

- Translation and localization.

- Personalization and behavioral targeting.

- Metadata strategy.

Yes, the content strategist will often assume responsibility for the activities and deliverables associated with each of these. But there are already several solid resources available about these practices, both online and offline. Content strategy processes and deliverables are less familiar and basically undocumented in the public sphere. So that's what I've focused on here.

## THAT'S IT. NOW YOU CAN START READING.

Okay. I think those are all of my disclaimers. I feel better. Thanks for your patience.

You can read the book now.

Enjoy.

# LEARN

Most web project schedules postpone content development until the eleventh hour. As a result, content quality is often seriously compromised. When we practice content strategy, we ensure that our web content is treated as a valuable business asset, not an afterthought.

# 1 SOLUTION

• • • • • • • • • • • • • • • • • • • • • • •

ON YOUR DAILY JOURNEY down the information highway, it's likely you spend a lot more time reading websites, search engine results, your mobile phone screen, and other online content than you spend reading print material. That means you're used to scanning a page for information and finding what you need (hopefully) within a matter of minutes.

In other words, you're used to instant gratification.

And so, in the spirit of getting you the information you need sooner rather than later, what follows are the top five ways to fix your web content.

If you only have the time and attention to read one chapter, make it this one.

## BETTER CONTENT STARTS RIGHT NOW

Your content can be better. Much better. And you don't need months of planning, a million dollars, and a new staff to succeed. In fact, if you can commit to these five efforts, you can radically improve your organization's web content in a fairly short amount of time:

1. Do less, not more.
2. Figure out what you have and where it's coming from.
3. Learn how to listen.
4. Put someone in charge.
5. Start asking, Why?

# #1: DO LESS, NOT MORE.

David Hobbs (WelchmanPierpoint) recently wrote, "Small websites are easier to manage than big ones. Since this is obvious, why don't more sites choose to be smaller?"*

Of course, it's rarely a matter of choice. A website tends to take on a life of its own, its growth fueled by new products and services, changing brand campaigns, multiple publishers, constantly-shifting executive priorities, user-generated content, and more. Beyond the website, there are company blogs, Twitter feeds, press releases, email communications, and so on. The Great River of Content flows freely, rapidly flooding our customers with too much information and drowning its keepers (web editors and content managers) in the process.

Why do we need all this content? What's the point?

**Generally speaking, your web content is useless unless it does one or both of the following:**

- Supports a key business objective.
- Supports a user (or customer) in completing a task.

If you assessed all of your current web content, how much of it would meet these two simple requirements? Ninety-five percent? Seventy-five percent? Less than half?

Typically when I ask this question of clients or seminar attendees, I hear a lot of rueful chuckling and see many shaking heads. Apparently, in most organizations, more content is perceived as more opportunity to sell, more support, more brand enhancement, more context, more everything.

But it's not.

---

*www.welchmanpierpoint.com/blog/web-diet-how-simplify-your-web-site

# WHY IS LESS BETTER THAN MORE?

I was recently working with a client who was very interested in reaching "critical mass" with the content on his website. I had no idea what he was talking about at first. His idea was that the more content he had:

- The better his search engine rankings would be.
- The more value he would provide to his online audiences.
- The more chance he had of creating "competitive differentiation" in his industry.

Yes, content can do a lot. However, the website my client was hellbent on creating would incur much greater costs than he could ever anticipate — in time, money, brand value, and customer satisfaction.

**Online, when it comes to informational, marketing, or promotional content, more is almost never more.** Instead of going for "critical mass," think about striving for "a whole lot less." Here's why.

## Less content is easier to manage

When we talk about content getting published online, we often refer to it as going "live." Interestingly enough, we seem to think that our content will magically continue to maintain itself, without care and feeding. But spend 30 seconds tooling around almost any website, and you'll find this is patently untrue. Dead blogs. Outdated product descriptions. Broken links. Irrelevant search engine results.

The countless ways in which our web content dies on the vine are painful, and sometimes dangerous. It's one thing to change our brand voice on one media channel but ignore our web content. It's another to neglect content that may expose us to legal action by a customer or competitor.

**So, by publishing less content, you will have less content to keep track of over time. It's a simple equation.**

## Less content is more user-friendly

Let's say you're ready to shop around for new auto insurance. You've written down a few top-of-mind insurance brands, including Allstate and State Farm.

For starters, you open a browser and type in www.allstate.com. And here is where you land:

Allstate.com

In the first three seconds of staring at this page, how confident do you feel that you'll find the information you're looking for? There are a lot of options to choose from. It's pretty overwhelming. (And, if you're like me at all, you hate to feel overwhelmed.)

Now you decide you'll give the Allstate site search engine a try. You go to the search box and type in *types of insurance*. Here are your results:

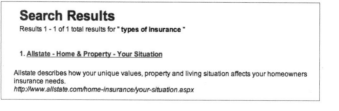

Wow. One result that has nothing to do with figuring out which kinds of car insurance you need. Talk about worthless.

How do you feel now? Frustrated? Resentful? Like leaving?

Too much content means information is harder to find. And that means it's harder for a customer to make a decision in favor of your product or service.

By contrast, take a look at State Farm's home page:

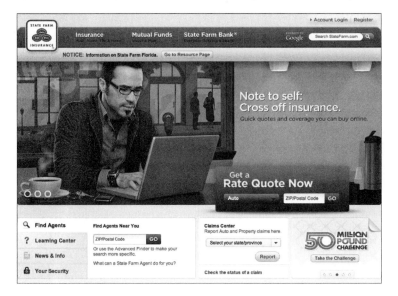

Clean. Concise. No-nonsense. You're in, you're out. And you're happy.

## Less content costs less to create

How's that for a forehead-slapper?

**By prioritizing useful and relevant over "wouldn't it be cool" and "just in case," you will magically dismiss at least half of your web content projects.** That means you'll free up time and money for things like planning and measurement, two content-related tasks that often get short shrift in the race to do more online.

How can you begin to scale back on content? Ensure that your website content maps back to key business objectives and user goals. Create a web editorial calendar that specifies when and why new content will be published. And, moving forward, stop creating so much "just-in-case" content.

# #2: FIGURE OUT WHAT YOU HAVE AND WHERE IT'S COMING FROM

Content strategy is a complicated undertaking. Planning to create, deliver, and govern content requires input from multiple sources, many of which are human beings. And that means it's messy.

**If you don't know what content you have now, you can't make smart decisions about what needs to happen next.** And to accurately assess your current content woes, you need to conduct a *content audit*, which is an assessment of your web content. People conduct content audits usually in preparation for a website redesign or for migrating content to a new content management system (CMS). It calls for an accounting of all currently published web content, often recorded in an Excel spreadsheet that details specific attributes of the content.

Content strategist Hillary Marsh offers her take on the subject:

> A content audit is sometimes known as a content assessment, or content inventory. Sometimes there is a distinction between the cataloging of all content and the evaluation of content. (To quote information architecture expert Christina Wodtke, an inventory is "what's there" and an assessment is "is it any damn good?")*
>
> No matter what the label, there needs to be both a cataloging and an assessment done for the content; often, the assessment is done a bit later.*

In this book, we use the terms quantitative content audits (cataloging data-based content attributes) and qualitative audits (an analysis of content quality and relevance; what Marsh refers to as "assessments"). If you're dealing with a few hundred pages of content, you can and should take this on immediately. If you're a larger organization, an enterprise-wide content audit may simply be impossible to take on all at once. But that doesn't mean it shouldn't happen.

For more information about how to conduct a website content audit and analysis, see *Chapter 4, Audit.*

---

*www.contentcompany.biz/articles/content_audit.html

# #3: LEARN HOW TO LISTEN

When doing discovery and research that will inform your content strategy, it's critically important to do equal amounts listening and talking. Why? A few reasons:

- **In any organization, responsibility for content is shared.** Your key content players aren't just the people who create content. Content owners actually include several roles and responsibilities: requesters, providers, creators, reviewers/approvers, and publishers. They all have daily needs and challenges that deserve to be heard and considered as you develop your content strategy.

- **No one knows better what your customer needs than your customer.** Although many of us truly believe we have the line into what our end users *really* want from us online, we can't really know unless we ask them.

So before you start handing down content requirements, processes, and standards from on high, do some serious listening. What you hear can and should inform your recommendations. After all, you're not creating plans for some alternate reality in which everything perfectly unfolds according to The Strategy. You're planning for human beings and their ever-shifting needs and desires, also known as the real world.

One quick note: Just because an employee or a customer asks for something does not mean it should be automatically delivered upon. Yes, you want to capture useful information to inform your content strategy, but sometimes it's enough simply to *ensure that people feel heard*. It's amazing what just a little acknowledgement and empathy will do.

# #4: PUT SOMEONE IN CHARGE

Who owns your web content?

Typically, I get one of two answers to this question:

- Lots of people
- One person, except that person is really just an order taker for content requests

In other words… no one. No one owns the web content.

Here's where we turn to the world of print publishing for some insight. Have newspapers been coming together day after day, year after year under distributed publishing models with no executive editorial oversight? Does a magazine make it to press thanks to a staff of writers whose marching orders are to acquiesce to every "emergency" content request?

Your organization needs to have an empowered, informed individual who is The Person in Charge of All Things Web Content. This doesn't mean this person needs to be solely *responsible* for all web content creation, delivery, and governance. It means that this person is charged with the same duties as an editor-in-chief (or executive editor) is for a print publication.

An editor-in-chief (EIC) is responsible for maintaining a very close eye on your content—what needs to be created, how it will get online, and what happens to it once it's live. This person is also often tasked with the day-to-day oversight of content standards and processes. And that makes this role invaluable to any organization.

For a more detailed description of the EIC role, see *Chapter 11, Maintenance.*

## #5: START ASKING, "WHY?"

I'll keep this last one brief.

A content strategy can accomplish all sorts of delightful things. But the most exciting thing of all is that **the process of developing a content strategy will force your organization to examine its reasons for delivering content online.**

Do any of these statements sound familiar?

> "This needs to go on the home page."

> "We should be on YouTube."

> "I need this series of brochures converted for the web."

> "We have to put our new mission statement in the About Us section."

> "Let's write another dozen articles next month."

> "We have to launch a blog."

Oh, really?

Why?

In our desire to deliver—to our employers, our clients, our customers—
we often race right past strategy and into execution. It's not that we're
not interested in doing the right thing. It's simply that we're under such
constant pressure to show results, to demonstrate value, to do *something*,
that we're programmed to hit the ground running the minute a request hits
our inbox.

Requests for web content pose an especially unique challenge because
web content is (or should be) easy to publish. You want a blog? There are
thousands of free blogging platforms that will sign you up in seconds. How
about a video series? YouTube and Vimeo are waiting for your upload. Need
a website? Again, everyone from Google to WordPress is happy to oblige.

So, yes. This is our reality. Literally, anyone can create and publish content
online. **But people, when it comes to your business, just because you** *can*
**doesn't always mean you** *should.*

Don't be distracted by hyperbole. Be cautious about the next bright, shiny
social media channel. Measure blue sky ideals against the realities of time
and money. Plan for content with care.

And don't ever hesitate to ask "Why?"

## THIS IS ALL A GOOD START

But it's only the beginning.

It's time for a change. It's time we all recognize, divide, and conquer the
multiple roles associated with planning for, creating, delivering, and governing useful, usable content.

That's what this book is about.

If we don't work together to make this fundamental shift—if we don't learn
to approach content strategically, as a critical business asset—we'll keep
underestimating the time, budget, and expertise it takes to do content right.
We won't clearly define and defend the process to our companies and clients. We'll keep getting stuck with 11th-hour directives and fix-it-later copy
drafts. And we'll keep on delivering subpar, inconsistent, irrelevant content.

It doesn't have to be this way.

Content strategy can help.

# 2 PROBLEM

FOR WEB CONTENT TO BE SUCCESSFUL, it needs to meet users' needs and support key business objectives. But visit any website, and you'll discover that much of the content doesn't remotely accomplish either of these goals. It's unnecessary. Overwritten. Irrelevant. In the way.

It's not that companies don't want to deliver useful, usable, persuasive web content. It's that most of us simply lack the process, tools, and resources to get content right. And yet, the web is content. Content is the web. Doesn't it deserve more of our time and attention?

## THE TRUTH HURTS, BUT PAIN IS GAIN

There are several problems that have contributed to our current web content crisis. This chapter will shed light on some the most prevalent ones. When you understand where the challenges are, you can better target where to implement solutions.

Here are some of the main obstacles that lie between our organizations and better content:

- Content isn't easy.
- No one owns the content.
- You never meant to be a publisher.
- Content is seen as a commodity.
- Our standards for content are really, really low.

Let's discuss.

# CONTENT ISN'T EASY

When we think about the content development process, here's how many of us (including and especially project managers) tend to think of it:

1. Concept

2. Create

3. Revise

4. Approve

In reality, dealing with the web content lifecycle looks a lot more like this:

1. Audit
2. Analyze
3. Strategize
4. Categorize
5. Structure
6. Create
7. Revise
8. Revise
9. Revise
10. Approve
11. Tag
12. Format
13. Publish
14. Update
15. Archive

The logistical complexities of the content lifecycle are a surprise to many. But, believe it or not, the inherent messiness of content starts well before it ever arrives at your content management system (CMS).

Here are some of the more intangible reasons content can be such a chore:

- Content is an unknown.
- Content is political.
- Content is time-consuming.

Each of these reasons is worth a closer look.

## CONTENT IS AN UNKNOWN

People often begin web projects with some fairly vague ideas about what content they have and what content they think they need.

To identify content needs, project owners hold meetings, send out email surveys, create "wish lists," and possibly even start to do some high-level information architecture.

To figure out what content they already have, perhaps someone thinks to gather content that exists outside of the web. Sometimes they'll collect a pile of print materials or dump hundreds of PDFs onto the project management server. And maybe, just maybe, project owners will even go so far as to audit their website content.

Unfortunately, drafting initial content requirements is only the tip of the iceberg. It's the content audit and analysis that will bring the size of the mountain into clearest relief. Climbing the mountain isn't easy. But the views are well worth it. (For more information, see *Chapter 4, Audit* and *Chapter 5, Analysis*.)

copyright 2008 Kevin Cornell

How do you eat the elephant in the room?

## CONTENT IS POLITICAL

When we wait until the last possible moment to ask for stakeholder input, stakeholders panic. And get defensive. And irritated. And possibly even straight-up angry. For example:

- The information architect hasn't seen this copy since it was "lorem ipsum" in the wireframes, and if she'd known it was going to say THAT, she would have totally taken a different approach.

- Marketing needs to sit down with you to ensure brand, messaging, and word usage are consistent with current campaign and style guidelines. (Which, didn't you hear? Those changed again three weeks ago. Here's the new 100-page manual.)

- The business owners, by the way, aren't really too happy with the direction marketing is taking with this new campaign. They're totally missing the boat on at least 14 key benefits, here. Can you take a stab at incorporating those benefits into your copy?

- Legal is sick and tired of the way everyone seems to be willfully ignoring the fact that we are *required by law* to include this 800-word disclaimer on every page that mentions this one particular service. They would prefer to see it at the *top* of the page so that no one will miss it. While they're at it, they have some input about the way you've phrased a few hundred sentences.

- By the way, CMS is going to need two months to enter all this content into the CMS now, not two weeks. This is a lot more than they expected. Sorry.

Yikes.

Who's in charge, here?

Without an empowered, informed content "sheriff" at the table, no one is. It's the wild west of content development, the place where all bad content is born, the place we all want to run screaming from, except launch is in two weeks and we just need to get the damn thing live, no matter what.

## CONTENT IS TIME-CONSUMING

We can either keep wishing that web content didn't take so much time to do right, or we can start planning for it accordingly.

Let's say you're a customer service manager, and you've been appointed a content reviewer for the "Support" section of your company's website redesign project. You're told this is an honor, because you really "get" customer service at your company. Hooray! You also know the project kicked off sometime last quarter, but you haven't heard much about it since then.

At 2:00pm on a Tuesday, an email arrives in your inbox. It's from the website project manager. There's a red flag beside the subject line, which reads, "ALL COMMENTS DUE 5:00PM WEDNESDAY (TOMORROW)." You open the email, and attached to it is a Word document entitled "Support.doc".

You open the document. It's 225 pages long.

On what planet is any normal human being going to be able to give this document a fair, careful, considered review over the next 27 hours?

And this is just the review process. Imagine how long it took a web writer (or team of web writers) to build out this document, research the topics, write about them in a manner that accommodates online readers, and optimize each page for search engines.

And this is just one section of the website.

Look. No matter what your job is, I'll go ahead and assume that you have a lot to do. And, unless you're one of the very few professionals out there who are dedicated full-time to thinking about, creating, and overseeing web content, content is something you do in addition to a million other things.

When we plan for the time to do content right, we can actually produce quality content that's meaningful to our audiences. For any organization, that would be an immediate online competitive advantage.

## NO ONE OWNS THE CONTENT

One of the biggest problems driving this sorry state of affairs is simply that no one is really sure who *owns* the content in an organization. Is it marketing? Subject matter experts? The agency? IT?

In most organizations, no one actually *does* own the content. No one is truly empowered to set policies and standards. No one is acting as your content's "executive editor," ensuring accuracy, timeliness, consistency, clarity, relevance, and style.

When no one owns the content, priorities clash and compromises are made. User needs are marginalized in the rush to alleviate stakeholder concerns and fulfill multiple, often unrelated internal requests.

| | MAY PRIORITIZE... | MAY NEGLECT TO CONSIDER... | IMPACT ON CONTENT... |
|---|---|---|---|
| **Business** | Budget/ROI<br>Schedule<br>Deliverables | User experience<br>Actual time to develop<br>Project risks | Content doesn't meet user needs<br>Missed deadlines delay project completion |
| **Marketing** | Talking about key features and benefits<br>Search engine optimization<br>Ability to measure response | Audience's priorities<br>Customer-facing copy<br>Governance planning | Content is more promotional than educational<br>Writing suffers from "marketing speak"<br>Content is launched then neglected |
| **Advertising** | Campaign-driven creative<br>Highly interactive features<br>Web 2.0 tools | Usability<br>Project impact<br>Measurement | Content is more flash than substance<br>Content is delivered in animation or graphics that can't be indexed or measured |
| **User Experience** | Audience needs and desires<br>Research<br>Visual design | Current state content analysis<br>SEO considerations<br>Planning for content | Business content objectives are overlooked or marginalized<br>Desired content can't be completed by project launch date due to lack of source material, time, or budget |
| **Information Technology** | CMS or development requirements<br>Production workflow | People involved in the content creation process<br>Brand and messaging | Content may be published with a "fix-it-later" plan<br>Final published content may not adhere to visual or editorial brand standards |

When it comes to web content, everyone has something to say. Whether or not all of these people's input and requests should be honored is a different story. If no one owns the content, you'll end up with a free-for-all that seriously compromises your content quality, consistency, and effectiveness.

# YOU NEVER MEANT TO BE A PUBLISHER

Only when we embrace our identities as publishers will we be able to commit to the necessary infrastructure to care for our content as a strategic business asset.

For years, we've been spending millions of dollars on strategy and research, user experience design, visual design, and technical platforms. In other words, we've invested in everything we need to build the online vehicles for our content.

And yet, strangely, it's the content that gets left until the last minute. It's the main reason projects are delayed or even abandoned. It's an afterthought, a nuisance.

Why? Because most of us haven't yet realized that we're actually in the publishing business.

In the mid-1990s, we all woke up one morning to discover that, suddenly, we were expected to establish an online presence for our organization *right now*. No one asked for it. No one planned for it. But almost overnight, if we wanted to build or maintain credibility as a viable, trustworthy organization, we needed a website. Period.

So, we did our best. We designed, wrote, coded. Websites were launched. Ecommerce took flight. Web-related professions exploded—in design, marketing, PR, software, systems, metrics, and more.

It took some time for us to embrace being in the website business. Then the online media business. The blogging business. The Web 2.0 business.

But here's the deal. The moment you launch a website, you're a *publisher*. The moment you begin a blog, send an email, participate in social media, build a widget, even show up in search engine results… you are a publisher.

Publishers plan far in advance which content they will create. They have established, measurable processes in place. They invest in teams of professionals to create and care for content. They would never think of starting with design and then cramming content in at the last minute.

Like it or not, this is your job now. Web audiences demand useful, usable content. If you don't deliver, they will leave. And in order to deliver, you need to make content a priority. You need to think like a publisher.

## CONTENT IS SEEN AS A COMMODITY

One of the first times I spoke publicly about the need for content strategy, an audience member raised his hand and said, "If you want people to see content as an asset instead of a commodity, maybe you need a new word to describe content. I mean, when I think of 'content,' I think of piles of useless crap."

To which I replied, "So what you're saying is that you're part of the problem." (Cue applause.)

To be fair, I understand where he was coming from. After all, there are approximately umpteen million pages of content currently published online. With all that content, surely we don't need to worry about creating more, right? We can just go *get some*. I mean, it's probably already on our site, even. Somewhere. It just needs a little freshening up.

Or else we think that maybe, just maybe, other people are out there generating content that might be of interest to our audiences. We can aggregate it. Filter it. Republish it. For *free*.

Seriously. Why spend money on something that already exists everywhere online?

**Because useful, usable content is not a commodity.**

## THERE ARE NO SHORTCUTS.

Creating useful, usable content requires user research, strategic planning, meaningful metadata, web writing skills, and editorial oversight. It requires people. With experience. And insights. And judgment. It requires planning. And input. And time. And money.

It will not happen automatically.

Done well, content can build your brand, close the sale, improve retention, and win loyalty. Done poorly, it will cause you to lose your audiences' attention and trust.

Content should be your first thought. Not an afterthought. There are no shortcuts. No matter what you've read, no matter what the "experts" are telling you:

- Aggregation doesn't equal differentiation.
- Users will not magically generate your content for you.
- You can't buy effective content on the cheap.

Let's discuss.

## Aggregation does not equal differentiation

**To truly differentiate yourself online, you must offer content that specifically and authentically embodies your brand.** Your content must be unique to your organization, in topic and tone. Your content must help your audience *do* something—better, smarter, and with greater ease.

Developing quality content isn't easy. So to some organizations, automatic aggregation of content (via RSS feeds or back-end algorithms) seems like a smart, painless alternative to the complicated, time-intensive, ongoing content creation process.

ALLTOP.COM, content aggregation: Been there, done that.

Similarly, the idea that we can pay to publish syndicated content under our own brand umbrella is wholly appealing. Sign on the dotted line, and fresh content will be delivered daily to your customers, courtesy of custom publisher number nine.

None of these tactics are inherently a bad idea. In fact, one or all of them might be right for your organization to employ. **But don't mistake these tactics as your answers to a long-term content strategy.** Simply achieving "critical mass" of content—on your website, in your RSS feed, on your blog—does not necessarily deliver any sort of real value to your audience. Or, for that matter, your business.

Quality, relevant content can't be spotted by an algorithm. You can't subscribe to it. You need people—actual human beings—to create or curate it.

## Users will not magically generate your content for you

Although "user-generated content" may sound like "content you don't have to create," unfortunately there's a catch: You can't always depend on your audience to deliver the goods.

I've worked on many, many web projects that included launching a "community forum." I put this phrase in quotes because launching a forum does not in any way guarantee the creation of a community. Just because you build it doesn't mean they're going to come.

For example: Let's say you own a technology company, and you're looking for ways to save money on phone-based customer support.

Your website support section has been sorely neglected for years. But rather than investing the time and money in researching, organizing, rewriting, and maintaining your support content (expensive and resource-intensive), you decide to launch a forum so that your customers can help solve each other's problems (low-cost and, you believe, low-maintenance).

The forum launches. A few customers show up and pose questions. No one answers them, so your staff does. More questions trickle in. But with so few posts, and so few visitors, the forum feels like an empty restaurant, or a lame party that no one went to. Within a few months, the "last post" dates are looking old and tired. And your phone support costs haven't decreased by a cent.

What went wrong? Beyond the forum launch, there wasn't a plan. No one considered how to advertise or seed the forum, let alone drive user adoption.

**If you're considering ways in which user-generated content can help you achieve business objectives and meet your end users' goals, be very realistic about the fact that it's hard work to make it work well.** It can happen. But it's neither cheap nor automatic.

Speaking of cheap...

## You can't buy effective content for $4

Brain Traffic web writer Elizabeth Saloka wrote a blog post titled, "Bangalore, We Have a Problem" that sums things up quite nicely:

> I've just stumbled on a company called Niche Writers India that offers web content for $4. Four. Dollars. That's, like, a sandwich. A gas station sandwich.

> Since when did web content become a cheap commodity? We're not talking about zipper togs and baby socks! We're talking about communication. Often, very technical and advanced communication.

> A sample of what you can expect for your four dollars:

> "Niche Writers India is the core when it comes to writing and this is what our clients feel about our content writing services expanding to various domains and collaterals. We have bubbling, energetic and youthful warp and woof of writers!"

> ... Niche Writers India, though not in the manner it intends, makes a compelling case for the value of a good web writer. Hopefully after seeing this site, would-be value shoppers will decide to invest (more than $4) in their content.

Hopefully.

Of course, if you're comparison shopping based on price alone, you may be willing to sacrifice some degree of quality in order to save money on content creation (or syndication). This actually happens a lot, and not just because content is undervalued or perceived as a commodity. It's because many of us simply don't know what really effective content looks like.

# OUR STANDARDS FOR CONTENT ARE REALLY, REALLY LOW

It's far too easy to find examples of bad web content. And it can be extraordinarily difficult to find the good stuff.

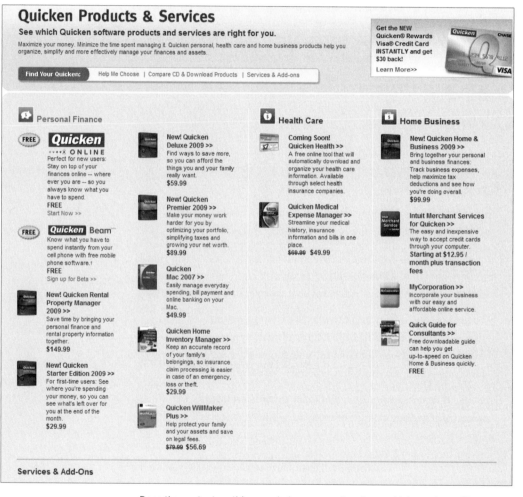

Does the content on this page help me see *at a glance* which product will most likely help me manage my personal finances?

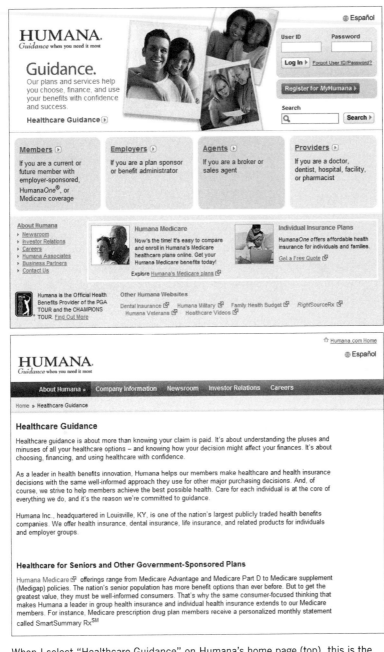

When I select "Healthcare Guidance" on Humana's home page (top), this is the information I get (bottom). Does this content deliver on Humana's promise to help me "choose, finance, and use [my] benefits with confidence and success"?

When poor content is so prevalent online, it's easy to relax into thinking ours only needs to be marginally better to stand out. When major brands aren't investing in their web content, why should we?

High-quality web content that's useful, usable, and enjoyable is one of the greatest competitive advantages you can create for yourself online. Check out Babycenter.com. Cancer.org (American Cancer Society). Kodak.com. These sites have all put killer content in the center of their online strategies.

You can, too.

## THESE PROBLEMS ARE NOT WITHOUT A SOLUTION

If you're reading this book, you're ready for a change. You're tired of seeing content marginalized or ignored in the web design process. You value quality content as central to designing a successful user experience. You're ready to undertake the many challenges associated with creating, delivering, and governing useful, usable content.

We need a new model for how we consider and care for web content. And at the heart of that model lies content strategy.

# 3 DISCIPLINE

WHAT IS CONTENT STRATEGY? Is it a practice? A document? A marketing plan? An umbrella term for a mishmash of quasi-related activities and deliverables?

What does it look like? Who's responsible for it? How is it implemented? Can we measure its success?

I mean, seriously. Do we really need content strategy?

Yes. Yes, we do.

## CONTENT STRATEGY'S TIME HAS COME

Since the web began, we've all been taught that web content is really somebody else's problem ("the subject matter expert can do it," "we'll hire a contract writer," "the users will generate it"). So, no one really worries about content until the last minute.

Do you think it's a coincidence, then, that web content is, for the most part, crap?

No one is asking the scary, really important questions about the content, such as, What's the point? or, Who cares? No one is talking about the time-intensive, complicated, messy content development process. No one is overseeing the care and feeding of content once it's out there, clogging up the tubes and dragging down our search engines.

That's where content strategy comes in.

In this chapter, we will:

- Define content strategy.
- Discuss content strategy processes and deliverables.
- Explore who does this work.

# CONTENT STRATEGY, DEFINED

Content strategy is the practice of planning for the creation, delivery, and governance of useful, usable content.

Let's break it down.

- **Content** includes text, data, graphics, video, and audio. Online, it's shaped and delivered by countless tools (such as animation, PDFs, streams, and so on).
- A **strategy** is a holistic, well-considered *plan* for obtaining a specific goal or result.

Often, when people talk about content strategy, they're talking about what they plan to deliver online, and where. In this context, people may discuss a content strategy as being made up of, for example:

- A series of educational articles.
- A full-service, online knowledge base.
- A sponsored YouTube channel.
- A blog by the CEO.
- A Twitter account.

**These tactics, when combined, do not make up a strategy.** They're just a bunch of tactics. A strategy is a carefully considered, well-articulated plan of action, achievable and executable. It's a roadmap that gets us from where we are now to where we want to be.

**Content strategy plans for:**

- **Creation.** What content will be created and why? How will that content be structured and found? Where will the content come from? Who will be in charge of creating it?

- **Delivery.** How will content get online? Who will review it, edit it, approve it, load it? What goes into phase one, phase two, and so on? How and where will you deliver content to your users? Which tools and data will ensure your users will find it?

- **Governance.** Who cares for the content after it goes live? What's the plan for adding, updating, and archiving content? What are the policies, standards, and guidelines by which content will be evaluated?

## BUT WAIT, THERE'S MORE!

In her groundbreaking article, "Content Strategy: The Philosophy of Data," Rachel Lovinger said:

> The main goal of content strategy is to use words and data to create unambiguous content that supports meaningful, interactive experiences. We have to be experts in all aspects of communication in order to do this effectively.*

Lovinger's article was the first to shed light on content strategy as a viable, valuable field of practice. Her vision of "unambiguous content that supports meaningful, interactive experiences" is an inspired call to action for content strategists everywhere.

However, I question her assertion that content strategists need to be "experts in all aspects of communication." That's a fairly tall order. In my opinion, there are simply far too many "aspects of communication" for a solitary content strategist to truly claim deep expertise in all of them. Instead, I think there are a number of content-related disciplines that deserve their own definition, by turn.

### Online messaging and branding

Online messaging and branding professionals specialize in defining what the "story" is behind the content. They answer questions such as: What are your brand values and attributes, and how will they inform the content? What do you want the user to learn or know after reading your web content? Do we say different things to different users? Do we talk to the same user differently depending on his current task or length of relationship with the organization?

---

*www.boxesandarrows.com/view/content-strategy-the

## Information architecture

Information architecture involves the design of organization and navigation systems to help people find and manage information more successfully. It's typically considered a subset of user experience design, with a focus on content categorization, user flows, labeling, and so on. These days, most information architects don't dig deeply into specific, detailed content requirements and structure beyond content models, site maps, wireframes, and page templates. An information architect with a clear focus on *the content itself* will define the content requirements for all pages or content components of a website. This includes structural, messaging hierarchy, source content, maintenance requirements, and so forth.

## Editorial strategy

Editorial strategy defines the guidelines by which all online content is governed: values, voice, tone, legal and regulatory concerns, user-generated content, and so on. This practice also defines an organization's online editorial calendar, including content lifecycles.

## Web writing

Web writing is the practice of writing useful, usable content specifically intended for delivery online. This is a whole lot more than smart copywriting. An effective web writer must understand the basics of user experience design, be able to translate information architecture documentation, write effective metadata, and manage an ever-changing content inventory.

## Search engine optimization

Search engine optimization is the process of creating, editing, organizing, and delivering content (including metadata) to increase its potential relevance to specific keywords on web and site search engines.

## Metadata strategy

Metadata strategy identifies the type and structure of metadata, also known as the "data about data" (or content). Smart, well-structured metadata helps publishers to identify, organize, use, and reuse content in ways that are meaningful to key audiences.

### Content management strategy

Content management strategy defines the technologies needed to capture, store, deliver, and preserve an organization's content. Publishing infrastructures, content life cycles, and workflows are key considerations of this strategy.

### Content channel distribution strategy

Content channel distribution strategy defines how and where branded content will be made available to users. (*Side note:* Please consider email marketing in the context of this practice; it's a way to distribute content and drive people to find information on your website, not a standalone marketing tactic.)

# UNDERSTANDING THE PROCESS

When does content strategy begin and end? How does it fit in with our established and emerging web-related best practices?

**Content is everywhere. It follows, then, that content strategy should be, too.**

Content strategy work starts even before the project objectives are defined. Its impact is felt well after the web content launches. And content strategy informs every other part of the web development process: design, development, SEO. The works.

But don't confuse content strategy with web strategy. It's not. Content strategy plays a very specific role in the web project process, clearly focused on content from start to finish.

## THREE STEPS TO CONTENT STRATEGY

The process for defining a content strategy is different from organization to organization. What follows is a high-level overview of the process I recommend to create a measurable, achievable content strategy.* As with any project, be sure you begin with a kick-off that helps set expectations for the project team and stakeholders. Define roles, explain the process, and gather whatever information you can before you kick your content strategy efforts into high gear.

---

*The content strategy process as documented in this chapter was developed by Melissa Rach of Brain Traffic.

## Step 1: Audit

A content audit is an incredibly important (but often overlooked) step when beginning any content project. By taking the time to figure out what content you have and whether it's useful (to your audiences, for your project objectives), you'll begin to understand the scope of your content needs.

A content audit can also serve as a terrific reference point when it's time to create new content by clearly showing what current content lives where.

(See *Chapter 4, Audit.*)

## Step 2: Analysis

The goal of the analysis phase is to define the objectives, assumptions, risks, and success factors for the project content—and get all of the project stakeholders to agree to them.

In this phase, the content strategist conducts an up-close, in-depth analysis of all internal and external circumstances that have impact on the organization's content. This includes anything that might inform or affect recommendations for content creation, delivery, and governance.

By helping to shape a project's strategic foundation, the content strategist ensures that content requirements are not being defined without clear recognition of how those requirements will impact project schedule, budget, or resources.

(See *Chapter 5, Analysis.*)

## Step 3: Strategy

During the strategy phase, the content strategist makes actionable, achievable recommendations for content creation, delivery, and governance—informed by the project goals. This body of recommendations is the content strategy document.

But simply recommending "here's how we should do this" isn't enough. Because the web content process touches so many areas of every organization, the content strategist also provides information about how the proposed recommendations will have impact on the organization and its users.

Lastly, the strategist needs to confirm that all stakeholders understand and align on the content strategy before moving forward.

Content strategy recommendations usually include:

- **What content do we need to create? Why?** These recommendations cover brand and messaging strategy, overall site structure, page-level content requirements, content types and formats, and so on.

- **How will the content be structured?** In collaboration with information architecture, content strategy recommends web content organization, template content structure, and page-level content design, including messaging hierarchy. Content designs may also call out source content locations, content gaps, open issues, and content maintenance requirements.

- **How will users find the content?** Recommendations may include web search and site search strategies, metadata requirements, possibly marketing/influencer outreach campaigns, and other ways to connect content with key audiences.

- **How will we get from here to launch?** These are detailed specifications for an inventory of recommended content requirements and gap analysis (what we have and what we need), workflow process, schedule, creation strategies—everything and anything that will support a successful, on-time, on-budget content creation process.

- **What's next once the content is "out there"?** These recommendations answer questions like: How will the site be maintained? What triggers updates or content removal? Who's in charge? How will editorial policies and standards be enforced?

(See *Chapter 6, Strategy*.)

## GETTING THE CONTENT DONE

Often, once the planning phase is complete, the content strategist will continue to play an important role in the production and implementation phases of a web content project.

### Content creation and delivery

The content strategist may collaborate closely with a web editor or web writer to oversee the creation, revision, and approval of all required content.

In the absence of a web editor or writer, the content strategist may also be called upon to create all necessary content.

During the project development (or "build") phase, the content strategist may work closely with developers to ensure metadata is appropriately structured and entered into the CMS. The content strategist may also participate in content quality assurance (QA) testing.

If content is being delivered outside of a CMS (for example, using social media platforms), the content strategist may create and implement a content "calendaring" system, or editorial calendar, that shows when and where content should be delivered.

**The content strategist is also the content problem-solver along the way.** If anything comes up that doesn't align with the strategy or schedule, he'll work with all the different players to get the content train back on track.

## Content governance

Ideally, an organization has an empowered web editor whose role is to oversee and facilitate the long-term governance of an organization's web content. In my experience, however, this is rarely the case.

A content strategist can offer a terrific starting point for organizations by creating a content maintenance plan, which may include not only a calendar of activities but also clear guidelines by which to assess content quality over time.

But before such a plan can be put in place, clear content standards and policies must be articulated and agreed-upon. These policies often are handed down by legal and regulatory departments. However, marketing, user experience, metadata, search engine optimization practices, and accessibility requirements and guidelines should also be taken into consideration. Working to adhere to and integrate these considerations is more than maintenance, or maintaining the status quo. It's governance, or leading content efforts with an eye on constant improvement.

As these content considerations shift and evolve—which they inevitably do, and quickly—the content strategist must stay closely attuned to new content opportunities and risks as they arise.

## CONTENT STRATEGY DELIVERABLES

The deliverables required for each project depend on the project objectives. Here are just a few examples of the deliverables for which a content strategist might be responsible:

- Message map
- Content inventory
- Gap analysis
- Site map
- Page tables
- Content template map
- Editorial strategy
- Content style guide (to include brand, format, usage, and legal requirements)
- Editorial (or process) workflow diagram
- Content management system architecture
- Metadata framework
- Taxonomy
- Content flow schematic
- Content model
- Content quality assurance tools
- Content production schedule
- Competitor content audit
- Content migration plan
- Content licensing evaluation report

# MEET THE CONTENT STRATEGIST

The content strategist is the person who is responsible for getting the content done for a project. This person:

- Is the advocate for the content throughout the project.
- Provides the background research and analysis that stakeholders need to make smart decisions about content.

- Creates recommendations for the content based on business and user needs.
- Works with the organization to implement the content online.

## JACK OF ALL (CONTENT) TRADES

In my experience, the content strategist is a rare breed who's often willing and able to embrace whatever role is necessary to deliver on the promise of useful, usable content. Ideally, especially on large or complex projects, the content strategist coordinates input from a team of experts, including IAs, web writers and editors, SEO practitioners, database managers, and subject matter experts.

## CONTENT STRATEGIST JOB DESCRIPTION

What follows is a sample job description for a content strategist. Of course, depending on the structure and needs of your particular organization, roles and responsibilities will vary.

> The **content strategist** is responsible for overseeing the successful identification and fulfillment of all web-related content requirements throughout the project life cycle.
>
> Collaborating closely with the information architect as well as other key project stakeholders (such as marketing, creative, technology, and business strategy groups), the content strategist is critical to defining the content needs of websites and applications.
>
> The content strategist will:
>
> - Gather, audit, and analyze existing content relevant to project requirements. (See *Chapter 4, Audit.*)
> - Collaborate with project leads to examine and analyze content "ecosystem" during the project discovery phase. (See *Chapter 5, Analysis.*)
>   - Determine projects' overall content requirements and potential content sources.
>   - Ensure team aligns on content objectives, assumptions, risks, and success factors.

- Develop content recommendations based on client business objectives and user needs. (See *Chapter 6, Strategy*.)

  - Coordinate and collaborate with a team of experts in IA, SEO, social media, database management, metadata, and anyone else who is assigned ownership of an online initiative.

  - Develop innovative solutions for content presentation, including content management, workflow, and maintenance.

  - Create taxonomies and metadata frameworks for grouping and tagging content.

  - Develop content indexes and mapping documentation for the new site.

  - Understand and help implement content accessibility standards according to national law and organizational policy.

- Shepherd content through the creation process. (See *Chapters 7, 8, and 9*.)

  - Oversee content migrations and prepare documentation to do so.

  - Work with database administrators to make necessary changes and updates.

  - Work with the web editor or web writer to oversee the development of all content to be included in the solution.

- Ensure there is a plan for maintaining and governing content post-launch. (See *Chapters 10, 11*, and *12*.)

## WHERE DOES INFORMATION ARCHITECTURE COME IN?

Information architecture and content strategy are really two sides of the same coin. To design successful content-driven user experiences, one role simply cannot succeed without the other.

Responsibilities do overlap. In fact, on small web projects, one person can play both roles. However, regardless of project size, it's usually most effective if a separate IA and content strategist work side-by-side.

Web professionals love to argue about which role owns what, where and when different roles should have decision-making authority, and so on.

This kind of discussion makes me crazy. Arguing over who owns what is a waste of time. Decide what's necessary, agree who will drive the effort, and get the work done.

No matter what, just make sure someone owns the content. While structure, taxonomy (content categorization), and nomenclature (menu labels) are critical to designing a successful website, without clear direction around the "meat" of the site—the content that will exist in every nook and cranny—these solutions will fall short, every time.

## WHERE SHOULD YOU START?

When it comes to our web content, it's easy to forget what we want, or even worse, to settle for less. Dealing with content takes time. It's messy, it's complicated, it's expensive, and it's never done.

But until we commit to treating content as a critical asset worthy of strategic planning and meaningful spend, we'll continue to churn out worthless content in reaction to unmeasured requests. We'll keep signing up for online content initiatives without pausing to ask why. Our customers still won't find what they're looking for. And we'll keep failing to deliver useful, usable content that people actually care about.

It doesn't have to be this way.

Content strategy will help you deliver content that inspires trust. Drives action. Builds loyalty. On time. On budget.

The rest of this book will show you how.

# PLAN

A strategy is a roadmap, a real-world plan to get us from where we are now to where we want to be. Take time to figure out the lay of the land. Explore your content ecosystems. Consider obstacles and opportunities. And just like that, your journey towards useful, usable content has begun.

# 4 AUDIT

WHEN I'M SPEAKING ABOUT CONTENT STRATEGY at conferences, I often ask my audience, "How many of you really know, in detail, what content you have on your website today and where it all lives?"

Even in crowds of 400 to 500 people, I usually see only one or two raised hands.

This is a problem.

Before you ever begin to brainstorm about which content you need, you must understand exactly what you have. Before you can decide where to focus your web improvement efforts (and allocate your budget), you need to know exactly what needs improving and why.

And to know these things, you need to do a content audit.

## SEEING IS BELIEVING

A web content audit is a full accounting of the content your organization currently has online.

Auditing web content—especially a large website—might sound tedious and time-consuming. It can be. But the results are extraordinarily valuable. In fact, an audit is your key tool for making a business case for any web content project.

When you finish this chapter, you'll understand the basics on how to:

- Create a content inventory.
- Do a quantitative content audit.
- Do a qualitative content audit.
- Approach specialized content audits.

Here's how it works.

# THINKING ABOUT SKIPPING THIS CHAPTER? DON'T.

So you think you know what's on your site, do you? Or you have the general idea, anyhow. So it should be easy to decide what to do next about your content. Right?

Do not—repeat, DO NOT—skip the content audit. This process is not just about listing URLs and page titles. It can provide an extraordinary amount of useful, enlightening information that's surprisingly valuable, especially when you're fighting for project support and funding.

## AUDIT ADVANTAGES

The biggest advantage of doing a content audit is proving to stakeholders the magnitude of content that needs to be considered. By using a spreadsheet to catalogue the number of HTML pages, downloadable PDFs, dynamic content modules, video clips, and other "live" web content for which your organization is responsible, you can wake up stakeholders to the harsh reality of their content woes.

A content audit can also:

- Serve as a reference for source (or existing) content during content development, which is highly efficient for writers and other content creators.
- Help you scope and even budget for a content project.
- Give you a clear understanding of what you have and where it lives, even if only to begin thinking about maintenance or content removal.

Because there are several different reasons for undertaking a content audit, it's a good idea to create clear goals for the audit before you begin. That way, you can tailor the kind of information you record in your audit to meet your needs or stakeholder interests. The more targeted the information in the audit is, the more likely you are to get the results you're looking for.

## YES, YOU REALLY DO NEED TO LOOK AT ALL THE CONTENT

It's important to look at *all* the content. This means getting beyond the home page and key landing pages. Why? Because the "deeper" content is often where your customers run into major problems.

In his book *Killer Web Content*, Gerry McGovern writes:

> I come across many websites where there is a well-designed top level with quality content. However, when you click down a few levels, everything changes—it's like walking out of a plush hotel straight into a rubbish dump.

You might have that website now. And although an audit of such a website may be painful, but it will show you—and your stakeholders—what needs to change.

## THE CONTENT INVENTORY: YOUR CORE AUDIT TOOL

To audit your current web content, click through every single page of your website and any other web content for which your organization is responsible, and record what you find. Then, you'll record your findings in a document called a **content inventory**.

A content inventory is nothing more than a spreadsheet that captures information (such as page title or URL) for each web page or content module you're responsible for creating, reviewing, or caring for.

Organize the content in your spreadsheet like an outline, ensuring that each page or module is clearly listed within its own site section.

Here's what a content inventory looks like:

### BRAIN TRAFFIC

BrainTraffic.com
Content Inventory: Current state website
June 15, 2009

| PAGE ID | PAGE NAME | SOURCE CONTENT |
|---------|-----------|----------------|
| 0.0 | Home Page | http://www.braintraffic.com |
| 1.0 | What We Do | http://www.braintraffic.com/what-we-do/ |
| 1.1 | Web Content Strategy | http://www.braintraffic.com/what-we-do/web-content-strategy/ |
| 1.2 | Information Architecture | http://www.braintraffic.com/what-we-do/information-architecture/ |
| 1.3 | Writing for the Web | http://www.braintraffic.com/what-we-do/writing-for-the-web/ |
| 1.4 | Training and Seminars | http://www.braintraffic.com/what-we-do/training-seminars/ |
| 2.0 | Our Portfolio | http://www.braintraffic.com/our-portfolio/ |
| 3.0 | Our People | http://www.braintraffic.com/our-people/ |
| 3.1 | Kristina Halvorson | http://www.braintraffic.com/our-people/kristina-halvorson/ |
| 3.2 | Amy Wallace | http://www.braintraffic.com/our-people/amy-wallace/ |
| 3.3 | Angie Halama | http://www.braintraffic.com/our-people/angie-halama/ |
| 3.4 | Angie King | http://www.braintraffic.com/our-people/angie-king/ |
| 3.5 | Beth Johnson | http://www.braintraffic.com/our-people/beth-johnson/ |
| 3.6 | Christine Benson | http://www.braintraffic.com/our-people/christine-benson/ |
| 3.7 | David Bowen | http://www.braintraffic.com/our-people/david-bowen/ |
| 3.8 | Elizabeth Saloka | http://www.braintraffic.com/our-people/elizabeth-saloka/ |
| 3.9 | Erin Anderson | http://www.braintraffic.com/our-people/erin-anderson/ |
| 3.10 | Josh Foldy | http://www.braintraffic.com/our-people/josh-foldy/ |
| 4.0 | Our Blog | http://braintraffic.typepad.com/ |
| 5.0 | Contact Us | http://www.braintraffic.com/contact-us/ |
| 6.0 | Privacy Policy | http://www.braintraffic.com/privacy/ |
| 7.0 | Sitemap | http://www.braintraffic.com/sitemap/ |

Then what? Well, it's up to you. The level of detail you want to capture in your audit will depend solely on your business objectives.

Let's take a look at different types of audits and why they might be used.

## QUANTITATIVE AUDIT: LOW-HANGING FRUIT

A quantitative content audit is basically an index of the content on your site. Just the facts. No frills. It's the easiest thing to do when you're trying to get your arms around what content you have and where it lives.

It's a good idea to do a quantitative audit when you want raw, undisputed data about your site content. **It also may be a "quick win" when you have a very limited timeframe to build a business case or prepare for an upcoming web project.**

For larger websites, Lou Rosenfeld (Rosenfeld Media) makes a great case for doing a "rolling content inventory," or a quantitative content audit that basically never ends:

Inventory your content on an ongoing basis. A content inventory is a process, not a deliverable. A content inventory shouldn't be something that you allocate the first two weeks of your redesign to; allocate 10 percent or 15 percent of your job to it instead.

... We've got to get used to the reality that ongoing, partial content inventories are likely to be far more cost-effective than trying to achieve the perfect, all-encompassing snapshot of our content. Traditional content inventory methods continue to make sense with small websites. But anyone who is trying to inventory the typical corporate, academic, or governmental site needs to stop tilting at the windmill of comprehensiveness.*

In general, a quantitative content audit is often the very first step in any content audit process. It can answer some or all of these questions:

- What content do you have?
- How is it organized?
- Who creates it?
- Where does it live?

Let's see how the answers to these questions will help inform your content strategy.

## WHAT CONTENT DO YOU HAVE?

In 2002, Jeff Veen (Small Batch) wrote a very concise blog post on how to conduct a quantitative audit of your website content:

Start at your home page. Identify the major sections of your site. For example, at adaptivepath.com, we've divided our site into these section: team, services, workshops, publications, and contact. If I were doing an inventory of [a] site, I'd start with [a] section, click in, and see what's linked from it. For each page that I visit, I'd record the information specified in the columns of the spreadsheet. I'd follow every link and navigate as far as I could through the site, making sure to gather data about every possible page on the site.†

---

* www.louisrosenfeld.com/home/bloug_archive/000448.html
† Doing a Content Inventory (Or, A Mind-Numbingly Detailed Odyssey Through Your Web Site) at www.adaptivepath.com/ideas/essays/archives/000040.php

You may want to note what kind of content each page or component is. This is particularly helpful if you're using a CMS with specified content types. Examples of different kinds of content include articles, marketing promotions, press releases, employee biographies, product information, frequently asked questions, and blog posts.

You should also record:

- PDFs and other downloads
- Videos
- Forms
- Functional pages (such as shopping carts and registration)
- … and so on

## HOW IS THE CONTENT ORGANIZED?

Whenever possible, it's most helpful to catalogue your web content like you would create an outline. List major website sections as your top-level "parent" (or primary) sections, and plug in pages and modules as "children" (or secondary, tertiary, and so on) sections or pages contained within each main section.

There are a few reasons to take the time to clearly document current-state content organization and hierarchy in your content inventory.

First, if you have a lot of web content, part of what's great about an audit is that you can finally figure out where it lives and how exactly it's organized. A content inventory can document that information in a way that anyone can review and react to it.

| PAGE ID | PAGE NAME |
| --- | --- |
| 0.0 | Home Page |
| 1.0 | What We Do |
| 1.1 | Web Content Strategy |
| 1.2 | Information Architecture |
| 1.3 | Writing for the Web |
| 1.4 | Training and Seminars |
| 2.0 | Our Portfolio |
| 3.0 | Our People |
| 3.1 | Kristina Halvorson |
| 3.2 | Amy Wallace |
| 3.3 | Angie Halama |

Second, if you don't already have a numbering system for your web content, it's a good idea to start one now. You can organize it in the same way you'd organize a document outline (1.0, 1.1, 1.1.1, and so on). By assigning a unique numeric ID to each page or component, you'll have a much clearer picture of exactly which content belongs to which section of your website. It's also incredibly helpful to have a system like this established when it comes time to link up the content inventory to other web project documentation; the number of a specific web page can correspond to the content strategy recommendations for that page, as well as the functional specifications for that page, and so on.

## WHO CREATES THE CONTENT?

At a high level, it's useful to note whether each piece of content on your site was created in-house, by a content partner (newsfeeds, articles, blog posts, and so on), or by your users.

For content created by your internal team, if you can, note who creates, approves, and publishes each piece of content. This information can be enormously helpful when you begin to ask questions about why certain content was done a certain way, or when you want to confirm it's okay to change or remove the content. We'll examine this topic in detail in *Chapter 7, Workflow.*

## WHERE DOES THE CONTENT LIVE?

If you're dealing with a very large site that's hosted on a number of different servers or platforms, take note of where the content lives within your technical infrastructure.

In your inventory, include a column for content location. Is the content in a content management system (CMS)? Static HTML? If so, what are the unique URLs? How is dynamic content (that is, content that is delivered in components versus entire pages) managed? Are people publishing content directly to a website from their desktops or servers?

Sometimes content may be stored in very strange places, so be prepared to do some digging.

## QUALITATIVE AUDIT: A DEEPER DIVE

Seeing what content you have and where it lives is helpful, but only to a point.

Many a site map has been constructed based solely on page titles. But when it comes to qualifying the usefulness of content, a page title doesn't tell you what the content actually says, or if it's useful to your audience. That's where a qualitative audit comes in.

**A qualitative audit analyzes the *quality* and *effectiveness* of the content.**

Your findings from this analysis provide insight to whether or not the content is useful, usable, enjoyable, and persuasive to your audience.

Some of the questions you might want to answer in your qualitative analysis include:

- What does the content say?
- Is the content accurate?
- Is the content useful?
- Is the content used by your audiences?
- Is the content written professionally?
- Is the content user-friendly?

## WHAT DOES THE CONTENT SAY?

A page headline or paragraph subheads are very easy to scan, and quickly. However, they won't necessarily tell you what information is actually contained on each page.

Headlines and subheads can be unintentionally misleading. Don't trust them. Instead, make the time to carefully read (or watch, or listen to) your content. Only then will you be able to accurately record what information is presented. Create a "topics" or "notes" column in your inventory to record what topics are discussed on each page.

## IS THE CONTENT ACCURATE?

Inaccurate or out-of-date content can mislead your users, be plain embarrassing, or, at worst, expose you to a lawsuit. Ask: Is the information correct? Is it up-to-date? Does it use your organization's most recent trademarks and copyrights? Do the links still work? You may need to engage subject matter experts in this part of the audit to help identify what's outdated or straight-up wrong.

In your content inventory, add a column for accuracy and create a rating scale. You might have a scale of 1 to 5 (with 1 being good and 5 being ridiculously bad.) Or, you might want a more descriptive list of options such as: good, updates needed, completely inaccurate. Whatever your scale is, keep it consistent so you can sort your spreadsheet later to summarize your findings.

## IS THE CONTENT USEFUL?

If your website content isn't supporting the successful fulfillment of your business objectives or your users' top goals, it's a waste of pixels.

Start by adding two columns to your inventory:

- Value to user.
- Value to business.

For each of these columns you can use a 1 to 5 ranking or high/medium/low… whatever works for you. Again, keep your scale consistent.

## IS THE CONTENT USED BY YOUR AUDIENCE?

How many people are visiting and reacting to your content? How can you know for sure? If you have accurate web analytics reports and analyses, take a look at them. Compare this to your usefulness scores. Are there connections? Trends? Discrepancies?

Work with a web analytics expert to figure out which metrics are meaningful in relation to the insights you're trying to gain.

## IS THE CONTENT WRITTEN PROFESSIONALLY?

It's often all too easy to spot content written by people who are not professional writers. When reviewing your content:

- **Check grammar, word usage, and spelling.** How would your eighth-grade English teacher grade this content?
- **Examine voice and tone.** Does the current voice and tone match up to your brand guidelines? At the very least, does it read the way you want it to sound?

- **Look at how the content is structured.** Does the page have short or long paragraphs? Subheads? Too many text links? Too few?

- **Verify the content lives up to web best practices.** Are links consistent with page titles? Are meaningful keywords used in page titles and subheads? Are sentences clear, compelling, and to the point?

To make your audit valuable, add a "writing" column to your inventory and create a consistent rating scale. And, if you don't have grammar and writing expertise, ask an experienced web editor or web writer to weigh in. They'd love to.

## IS THE CONTENT USER-FRIENDLY?

Depending on your organization, "user-friendly" may mean different things. Regardless, it's very important to consider your content from your user's perspective.

Consider the information. Is it focused on meeting customer needs, or is it all about your organization? Does it use internal buzzwords and acronyms, or is it written so that your target audiences will understand and relate to it?

By now you know the drill. Add a column called something like "user-friendliness" and create a consistent rating scale.

# SPECIALIZED AUDITS: BECAUSE CONTENT IS COMPLEX

The quantitative and qualitative audits are the core processes that you'll use to analyze your web content. But depending on your business and the goals of your audit, it's possible that you'll need to gather specific information about your content that's unique to your organizational mission or project objectives.

Here are a few good examples of what I call "specialized" audits. You can add these pieces to either a quantitative or qualitative inventory.

# SEO: IS THE CONTENT FINDABLE?

Although SEO is not the only consideration when creating "findable" content, it's most often the tactic we turn to (for now). There are two main issues to consider when analyzing the quality of your content findability:

- **Content findability.** How are your targeted keywords performing in web search engines? How is your internal site search engine performing and why?

  If you have a search engine optimization (SEO) strategy in place, you should have access to the list of keywords that are important to feature in page headers and body copy. You can add a column to your inventory to list which keywords appear on each page or simply rank whether the use of keywords on the page is appropriate.

- **Content readability.** Some SEO copywriters are guilty of loading content with so many keywords that it becomes overly redundant or even unreadable. Check to see that the keywords are worked into the content in ways that support meaning and clarity, not destroy them.

# METADATA: THE CONTENT BEHIND THE CONTENT

When you're analyzing your site content, remember that there's more to it than just the words on the screen, or video or audio artifacts. For content findability and management purposes, among myriad other considerations, it's a good idea to gather and analyze the metadata.

Metadata is "information about information." It's the attributes we assign to content that allow web search engines to index our content. Metadata is also what helps our site search engines and content management systems organize and deliver content when and where our users need it most.

What kind information about metadata you record depends on your needs, but a few things may include:

- What is the quality of the metadata for the page? (Add a column and rank it.)
- If you didn't include them in your SEO audit, what are the page titles, keywords, header tags, and page descriptions associated with the page or content? (Add a column and paste keywords in.)

In the analysis and strategy phases, you (or someone) should develop a metadata strategy for your new and improved content. No matter who's responsible for that strategy, their first question will be, What are the existing metadata schema? Be ready with the answers. Talk to whoever is currently responsible for metadata, find out what's been done to structure and maintain it (if anything), and document your findings.

## LOCALIZATION AUDIT: WHEN IN ROME...

If your site serves people in distinctly different regions, cultures, or countries, whether or not the content requires translation, it's very important to consider the localization (or attunement to cultural differences and perspectives) of your content, including:

- **Language translation.** Simply translating content from one language to another rarely achieves the desired effect. Nuance is lost, meanings are misinterpreted, homonyms are slaughtered. What might be misinterpreted in context of local slang, social norms, and societal values?

  Rank whether the translation accurately represents your business goals and user needs.

- **Cultural indicators.** Are the images, testimonials, and case study examples relevant and meaningful to your geographically targeted audiences? (For example, Jennifer and Jason might be common names used in case studies in the United States. Brazil or China, not so much.)

  Rank whether each piece of content is culturally on target or sticks out like a sore thumb.

If you don't have the language or cultural knowledge necessary, ensure that you have an expert, savvy cultural advisor or translator reviewing all content for any red flags.

# WRANGLING THE RESULTS

Once your content audit is complete, you should have a clear understanding of what content you have and (hopefully) where it's coming from. So, now what do you do with all that information?

You can take immediate action by removing or archiving content that is so egregiously bad that you can (or must) retire it immediately. At the very least, you can send your audit to anyone and everyone who needs to take a look at your content universe, in all its messy, messed-up glory.

These things will likely make you a hero, or least they will get people's attention. And once you have people's attention, you have the opportunity to present a business case for your web project or initiative. And any project or initiative worth its salt begins with in-depth analysis of all relevant information and circumstances, which in turn leads to informed, achievable recommendations.

Yep. The content strategy party has only begun.

# 5 ANALYSIS

• • • • • • • • • • • • • • • • • • • • • • • • • • •

NOW THAT YOU'VE DONE YOUR AUDIT, it's likely you have a ton of ideas about what to do next. Why not just jump right in?

Hold on there, chief. You've reached the most crucial, important point in your content strategy project life cycle. Take a deep breath, and let's talk calmly about what to do next.

Before taking any action, you must—repeat, MUST—take the time to ask important, pertinent questions about your content *and everything else* that could possibly have impact on its creation, delivery, and governance.

If you can understand the world in which your content lives, you'll be better positioned to make strategic recommendations that can actually be successfully implemented.

## NO TIME OR BUDGET FOR ANALYSIS? FIND IT.

When you're constantly being asked to deliver projects in less time with fewer people and smaller budgets, why isn't it enough just to decide what you want and dive in? How can you possibly slow down for content-focused research and analysis?

My question is, how can you *not*?

Your web content doesn't exist in a vacuum. Organizational goals, real-world resources, who your users are, what your users want, competitor activities, and many other factors all affect whether or not your web content will be successful.

One of the most valuable roles a content strategist plays on any project or editorial team is that of content analyst. By focusing on content and everything that has impact on it, directly or indirectly, the content strategist assumes ownership for recommendations about improvements to content-related processes and the end content product.

In this chapter, you'll learn how to answer the following questions, and why those answers are essential to your content strategy:

- Why are you doing this project?
- What's in your communication ecosystem?
- How does content happen?
- Who are your users, and what do they want?
- What are your competitors up to?
- Who else influences your users' opinions?
- Do current events affect your project?

## GETTING ORIENTED FOR THE ANALYSIS PHASE

The analysis phase of your content strategy efforts involves rigorous discovery work and, often, significant amounts of documentation. There's a lot to do, and typically little time to do it in. You have to know which questions to ask, and where to ask them. Can answers be found inside your organization? Are there outside factors and forces that might matter? Yes, and yes.

### LOOK DEEP WITHIN

In my experience, it's often the organization itself—people, processes, and policies—that gets ignored or glossed over in project discovery phases. Many assumptions are made that affect your content. Often, these assumptions are flat-out wrong, and they end up costing everyone time and money. By digging into the core objectives, current processes, and potential risks that exist within your organization, you can base future recommendations on reality, not assumptions. And that's always a better idea.

## LOOK OUTSIDE YOURSELF

Don't fall victim to the "navel-gazing" syndrome. You know, the phenomenon where organizations spend so much time thinking about themselves, they forget there's a real world outside with the power to bring them down. (This is also called "drinking your own Kool-Aid.") You'll need to do some work to connect with forces beyond your control that impact your content: user opinions, competitor campaigns, social and economic trends, and so on.

## AND, ULTIMATELY, GET ALIGNMENT

Doing all this research is one thing. Getting all of your stakeholders to align on your findings is quite another.

To make the analysis phase really worthwhile, once you've finished, you need to:

- Present your key findings to all of the key project stakeholders.
- Get the stakeholders to align on project objectives, assumptions, and risks the findings suggest.
- Give them a document they can reference in case they forget what they aligned on.

The analysis document—also called the **strategic foundation**—ends up serving as a stellar reference guide for the project. It clearly spells out the project's purpose, scope, business goals, and user needs. It can help focus resources appropriately, prevent scope-creep, and identify additional opportunities.

It's important to understand that your analysis findings are *not* your content strategy. In fact, the strategic foundation document shouldn't even include any recommendations for the future content. It simply summarizes and analyzes the resources, research, and circumstances that inform recommendations about the creation, delivery, and governance of your web content.

## AND NOW, LET'S PAUSE FOR A QUICK REALITY CHECK

These processes and documentation may be scaled according to project size and resource constraints. (Scaled, not skipped!) In fact, I've seen an effective analysis phase done in as little time as three days.

If you're short on time, figure out which activities and information are most valuable to your specific project. Just remember, every hour you spend in analysis will likely save dozens, if not hundreds, of hours during content creation, delivery, and governance.

All right. Now you should be somewhat oriented and ready to get cracking. Ready? Let's do this thing. Let's analyze.

# WHY ARE YOU DOING THIS PROJECT?

This might seem like an easy question to answer, but it usually ends up being a pretty complicated discussion.

Whether your organization is considering a blog, actively participating in chat forums, launching a Twitter account, or tackling an entire website redesign, the first thing you need to do is answer four deceptively simple questions:

- What is the business trying to achieve with this content?
- What do our users want and need from our content?
- How will we measure the success of our content?
- What can we do with our available time, talent, and budget resources?

When you answer these questions, you can create clear, achievable project objectives and success metrics. In fact, answering these questions is one of the main reasons for doing the analysis phase in the first place.

All of the information you gather throughout this phase is intended to help you and your stakeholders have a clear idea of what *is*, so you can decide what could *be*.

# KNOW THE DIFFERENCE BETWEEN GOALS, REQUIREMENTS, AND TACTICS

Defining project objectives can be a difficult and contentious process, but it doesn't have to be.

Let's say you're doing a big web redesign project. If you ask a room full of project stakeholders what their objectives are for the project, they'll probably give you answers that range from high-level concepts ("I want to increase sales") to detailed tactics ("I want a picture of the CEO on the home page"). They all think their input is important—and, in fact, many of their suggestions may indeed be legitimate and valid.

So why is it so difficult to compare these things to each other or rank them in priority?

**Because goals, requirements, and tactics are not project objectives.**

You'll make life easier if you separate stakeholder suggestions into four categories:

## Business goals

You can spot a business goal a mile away. It has impacts on the organization far beyond whatever your content project could achieve. A business goal includes phrases like: "increase revenue," "increase market share," "create employee efficiencies," "improve the customer experience," and so on.

Business goals are, of course, important. They're some of the key criteria you use to inform your project objectives. But they're not objectives.

## Tactics

Tactics are specific features, functions, or activities. Most often tactics are things people want to see on the site (such as the CEO picture, a blog, or up-to-date product descriptions). Tactics can also be behind-the-scenes activities (such as "change the database entry system," "move Lisa to editor," or "have all content approved by legal").

Keep close track of all the tactics your stakeholders suggest in a document your stakeholders can see. They'll feel heard, which is really half the battle when working to align people. And once you have your project objectives defined, you'll be able to prioritize the tactics people request.

## Requirements and restrictions

On every project there are some things that are non-negotiable… or, at least, you assume they are in the beginning:

- **Budget.** The perennial favorite.

- **Timeline.** Two weeks from yesterday.

- **Technology.** Don't wait until it's time for production to figure out what you're working with on the back end. Does the way the site is being programmed impact the way content needs to be submitted for development? What opportunities or restrictions exist within your current CMS? Do you have specific templates your content needs to fit? Is changing fields in the database off-limits?

- **Must-have tactics.** In some cases, there are tactical features and functionalities that simply have to be there for one reason or another. A clear example is customer help text on an e-commerce site. A foggier example is something like, "The CMO is hot about customer communities and she only agreed to fund this project if it included one." Yeah. It happens.

- **Legal requirements.** Privacy policies, footnotes, trademarks, and so on, and so forth, ad nauseam. What the legal department wants, the legal department usually gets. Talk to them early and often.

- **In-force agreements.** These are business agreements or contracts that may have impact on content recommendations. For example, if your organization has a co-branding agreement—say, Target and Isaac Mizrahi, or WebMD and the FDA— it's critically important to take all contractual, content-related requirements and guidelines into account. Don't wait until the "final" content goes to legal, assuming they'll take care of it. Dig into the agreements early in your discovery process.

- **Accessibility.** Is your web content accessible to people with disabilities? If the answer is "no" or "I don't think so," you have work to do. Many government websites are required by law to make content accessible. And major corporations have been sued because content wasn't accessible. To find out which accessibility laws, regulations, or policies may govern your content, visit www.w3.org/wai/policy.

None of these answers will necessarily be set in stone. Requirements and restrictions often change after the analysis phase is complete and your stakeholders have all the facts in front of them. But by completing this research and analysis, you'll always have some parameters to fall back on.

## Project objectives (real ones)

These are the suggestions and requests you're really looking for. Sometimes project objectives are obvious. Sometimes they take a lot of negotiations.

**Project objectives always:**

- Are specific to this project, but are comprehensive enough to apply to large parts (if not all) of your web content.
- Help to accomplish your overall business goals.
- Take into account your project requirements and restrictions.
- Help you measure and define project tactics.

For example, your project objectives may be to:

- Update our website to better reflect our stature as a dynamic industry leader.
- Create a web content structure that is flexible enough to accommodate our ever-expanding product list and our new social media campaign.
- Educate our users about our products and make it easy for them to buy online.
- Bring the website more in line with other websites in our corporate family.

## Divide and conquer

By dividing your stakeholder suggestions into business goals, tactics, requirements and restrictions, and project objectives, you're ensuring not only that every stakeholder gets heard but that they also understand what will happen to their suggestions moving forward. And, you get clear, actionable project objectives at the same time. Bingo.

## PROJECT OBJECTIVES ARE NO GOOD WITHOUT...

Project objectives alone can only get you so far. Once your objectives are established, you'll need to identify your project success metrics, assumptions, and risks.

## Success metrics

Success metrics, or key performance indicators (KPIs), take your project objectives one step further by establishing how you'll know if your project objectives are achieved.

## Assumptions

When you start your project, there are likely to be a few unknowns. Maybe you'll have to trust that the new database will be done on time to meet your deadline. Maybe you have to simply believe that a web editorial style guide will magically materialize.

Document these assumptions so people remember what they told you would happen at the time you defined your project objectives. If those assumptions change, you'll have a damn good reason to change objectives and requirements. And, no one can blame you. It'll all be documented.

## Identified risks

Every project has risks. Identify them early, so you can do what you can to mitigate them.

By including the risks in your analysis documentation, you're ensuring all of the stakeholders understand the potential pitfalls before they happen.

When the risks are identified up front, roadblocks become less scary. If you run into a problem, the entire team can work together to implement "plan B" instead of pointing fingers about whose fault it is. This way, each member of your team is responsible… and prepared.

# WHAT'S IN YOUR COMMUNICATION ECOSYSTEM?

When it comes to web content, people in externally-facing communications roles—marketing, advertising, PR, corporate, investor relations—usually have a strong opinion about web content. And they have good reason to. All communication initiatives and content are connected. The success of their projects (and yours) depends on sending consistent, cohesive messages to your target audiences, no matter where they are or when they receive them.

So, instead of ignoring or fighting your friendly communication compatriots, enlist them to help you figure out where your project lives in your organization's communication ecosystem.

## BRAND: HOW DO YOUR USERS THINK OF YOU?

The word "brand" means many things to many people. But one thing's for sure: *You* don't own your brand. Your brand is what users think and feel about your organization. And online, user ownership of your brand is even more transparent.

So when you're planning your content strategy, you'll need to consider how your brand will impact your new web content. You need to get clear on how you *want* your users to think and feel about you, and plan accordingly. The results of your research should be articulated as *brand values,* or a small number of descriptive behaviors that your brand should exemplify. (Examples of brand values are "inspiration," "education," "collaboration," or "innovation.")

To start, find out if there are any corporate branding initiatives underway. Document how your team will work within these guidelines… or if not, why not?

If your website or other web content is the catalyst for new corporate brand work (and it often is), or if your organization wants your site to introduce a brand, you've got work to do.

This obviously isn't a book about branding, but here's the bare minimum you can do:

- Find out what your audience thinks about your organization today, and what they expect from you. (This is your existing brand.)
- If you'd like your users' perceptions to change, define how.
- Identify your organization's competitive advantages and positive unique qualities.
- Create a plan to improve your users' perceptions by playing off your key strengths and unique qualities.

There's a heck of a lot more to it than that, but this should get you started. For more information on brand identity, check out *Designing Brand Identity: A Complete Guide to Creating, Building, and Maintaining Strong Brands* by Alina Wheeler.

### Guidelines and best practices

Is there a corporate brand style guide? If so, does it have content guidelines? Has anyone established web best practices that need to be followed? Find out and do your best to comply. Your users might not be aware of specific inconsistencies, but they'll notice when something doesn't match their idea of your brand.

### Voice and tone

Another related consideration is the voice with which your web content will "speak." Is it casual and chatty? Professional and clear?

Whatever brand characteristics your organization chooses, the way in which your messages are delivered—your online tone of voice—makes an enormous difference in the way your users perceive your organization and your messages.

Voice and tone are the most flexible components of your brand. Although the corporation has a voice all its own, the voice for your content will depend on your project objectives. For example, the corporate voice may be appropriate for investors and media relations, but not for a website focused on customer satisfaction, or for branded content on social media sites.

## MESSAGING: WHAT DO YOU WANT YOUR USERS TO KNOW?

Messages are simply pieces of information you give to the user. So for your web content project, you need to define what you want the user to learn from visiting the site—and what information they expect to get.

Every organization has overall messaging strategies, whether you've established them formally or not.

If you're in a large organization, there are likely multi-million dollar projects devoted to creating messaging hierarchies. Get insight from the messaging stakeholders about what your content messaging needs to accomplish.

If you're in a smaller organization, a web project might be the first time anyone has really thought about overall corporate and brand messaging. Hold a workshop or two with key staff to find out what kinds of things you'd like to tell your customers, and discuss what kinds of questions users want answered. (*Hint:* Ask your salespeople. They have these conversations every day.)

In your analysis document, make a preliminary list of the key messages you may want send to your users. Get everyone in your organization to agree that you're headed in the right direction.

## CHANNELS: EVERYTHING'S CONNECTED

Obviously, your web content is only one way to communicate with your customers. Other communication channels often affect the kind of content your user expects to see online. (For example, printed materials may refer to the website for "more information," or an executive blog may have links to specific content on your site.)

As a result, it's important to find out all of the other channels currently used or planned to communicate to your users, such as:

- **Public website(s):** What are all of your organization's public websites? (There are likely more than you think.)
- **Intranets/extranets:** Are no intranets/extranets associated with the organization that your users may access?
- **External social media activities:** Which "influencers" do you want your messaging to target? What types of content are most easily shared among social media participants? Where do you want to deliver your content? Where do you hope it gets picked up? Will you enforce copyrights, or will you release content under Creative Commons licensing?
- **Public relations and awareness:** How does the PR team work? Are there other awareness campaigns (for example, does your boss do a lot of public speaking)?
- **Print media:** Do you communicate to your users with brochures, spec sheets, or similar? If so, are users likely to see those materials before or after they see your web content? Do they refer to your project content?
- **Other traditional media (TV, radio, and so on):** Are there any times these media are used? If so, what for? Do you need to expect an influx of users to your content after a show airs?
- **Email campaigns:** Do you communicate regularly to your users via email? Will those emails link to your project content?

- **Advertisements/SEM:** Are there advertising campaigns currently underway? What about paid search placements? Do they link to your project content?

An effective way to think about this interconnectedness is to map out your website's "family tree." It really sheds light on how important it is not to publish, revise, or remove content without understanding which other online sources may point to that content as a solution or reference for potential customers.

## SOURCE CONTENT: YOU HAVE TO START SOMEWHERE

If you're planning to create original content for your site, consider first what content you already have. It's a heck of a lot easier to start from something that exists already. And chances are good you have quite a lot of content to start with. Using source content doesn't mean copying text or information word-for-word and pasting it onto a website. It means looking for ideas, facts, and features.

As you talk to your communication stakeholders or review your existing materials, note which ones might be helpful during the content creation process and what topics they cover. Be sure to review:

- Current web content (aren't you glad you did the audit?)
- Extranet content
- Print documents
- Video transcripts
- Customer testimonials
- … and so on

## SEARCH ENGINE OPTIMIZATION: THE MISSING LINK

Search engine optimization (SEO) is a field of practice that's constantly evolving to keep up with the way search engines index and categorize content. There are dozens of tactics to improve your web content search engine rankings.

True SEO requires a strategy, not just a tactic or two (like a sitewide rewrite that mucks up your content, thanks to overzealous keyword placement). In fact, there's a movement to begin considering *findability* as the desired outcome of your efforts. This focuses your work not just on playing the Google game, but also on helping your users find the right information when and where they need it. That effort may very well include improving your site search engine, which is always on everyone's to-do list but rarely gets done.

If there are SEO or other search-related efforts underway, be sure to capture them in your analysis document. They'll play an important role in informing your content strategy recommendations.

# HOW DOES CONTENT HAPPEN?

In organizations big and small, it seems like everyone has an opinion about web content, but no one is really sure whose job it is to assess requests and implement changes. So, it's best to establish early who's on the content team and how the content process currently works.

## ROLES: WHO'S DOING WHAT?

In most organizations, even small ones, roles that include responsibilities for web content are somewhat of a moving target. Or an unsolved mystery.

There are more than a few people who may be involved with your content from concept to publication:

- **Requesters** submit requests for web content to be created, updated, or removed.
- **Providers** are subject matter experts who own and manage source content—or who have the necessary information in their heads—that will be used by creators to develop web content.
- **Creators** are responsible for actually developing the content (text, graphics, audio, and video).
- **Reviewers/approvers** must be consulted about some or all of the content prior to its publication online. (*Note:* Not every reviewer will have the same "clout"—do your best to understand, from the approver(s), how and why reviewers must be consulted.)
- **Publishers** get the content online, via coding, a content management system, a wiki, a blog, or other technical wizardry.

- **Community managers** may be responsible for participating in online conversations via social media. Every comment they post, every press release they submit to a blogger, and every time they respond to a comment in a public forum, they are creating content that reflects your organization's values, personality, and positioning.

Who are these people? Which departments do they work in, and who do they report to? What are their skill sets? What do they want? What do they need? How can you help? Should you help? Are there interoffice politics involved that may affect content recommendations? All of these answers will inform your content strategy, as well as recommendations about the editorial workflow that will drive content creation.

## CONTENT WORKFLOW

From request to publication to archival (or not!), your web content follows a workflow. This workflow may or may not be standardized or even documented. Publishing content may be planned for, or it may be a recurring fire drill.

Regardless, the better you can understand how content moves from somebody's idea or requirement to getting online, the better position you'll be in to offer smart recommendations about how to create new workflow efficiencies.

For more on this topic, see *Chapter 7, Workflow.*

## MAINTENANCE AND OVERSIGHT

Web content never takes care of itself. In fact, it's renowned for its ability to die quickly on the vine. Once your content is published online, who owns it? How much of their time is dedicated to updating it? Who gets to decide when new things are added or archived?

For more on this topic, see *Chapter 11, Maintenance.*

# WHAT DO YOUR USERS WANT?

Your users are your target audiences, customers, members, readers, or anyone else you'd like to engage online. When it comes to content, what do they want?

You may *think* you know what they want. In fact, you may think you know what they need more than *they* do.

This, of course, is silly. While you may be an expert about your product or service, you most certainly cannot read your users' minds. Nor are you in any position to tell them what they want or need.

Why? Because online, you don't have a captive audience. You have a multitasking, distracted, ready-to-leave-your-site-at-any-time audience who has very specific goals in mind.

If your content doesn't meet those goals, and quickly, they will leave. Period.

Rahel Anne Bailie, principal of Intentional Design, is very passionate about ensuring the user experience strategy (that is, what you want your users to be able to achieve on the web). Here are her thoughts about planning for content:

> What does the *user* require to be able to have the best possible user experience?
>
> When [content creators] start saying, "We have to get all of our content to converge here; we need to integrate prices from that database into product descriptions from that database," then technical requirements emerge. But you need to start with user experience requirements, which will then drive the tech requirements.
>
> For example, "We will deliver PDF docs because that's how we've always done it." BUT—is that what people want?*

There are unlimited ways to get a good understanding of what users want. There are thousands of user experience design professionals who would like to help. Here are just a few tactics you can consider:

---

* The quoted paragraphs are from an email by Rahel Anne Bailie to Kristina Halvorson.

## USER RESEARCH

In order to really know what your users' goals are, you need to find a way to ask them. You also need to understand where they're coming from, who else they're talking to (competitors), what your audience segmentation is, and which messages will most likely convert and retain them. And that is user research.

For more ideas and information about user research, use cases, and personas, these are my favorite books:

- *Observing the User Experience: A Practitioner's Guide to User Research* by Mike Kuniavsky.

- *The Persona Lifecycle: Keeping People in Mind Throughout Product Design* by John Pruitt and Tamara Adlin.

- *Mental Models: Aligning Design Strategy with Human Behavior* by Indi Young.

## WEB ANALYTICS

One of the many revolutionary aspects of the web is that we are now able to measure with some precision how people interact with our content online. We can tell, to some extent, what content visitors are most interested in. And that information might surprise us.

This changed the game for marketers and advertisers. But with respect to content quality, many practitioners are flip-flopping with regard to which numbers matter, and whether we can make use of them.

That said, during research, the key thing to focus on is whether or not useful analytics are available, and if so, how they may inform your recommendations. We'll look more closely at analytics and content strategy in *Chapter 10, Measurement*.

For now, here are the main questions to focus on in this area.

### Which metrics are you using to measure content effectiveness, and why?

Your metrics—sometimes part of your web content's KPIs—will vary based on your organization's mission, products, and services.

As described in Eric Peterson's superior *Web Analytics Demystified,* sample metrics may include:

- Click-throughs
- Page views
- Site visits (or user sessions)
- Unique visitors
- Conversion rates
- Abandonment rates
- Attrition
- Loyalty, frequency, and how recently users have visited the site

I'd also add Google page rank (that is, figuring out on which page of results your content appears when users search using specific keywords) here, as well as how the site's content is mapping to and facilitating your business objectives.

If there is solid analysis available in addition to these metrics, great. Include findings and trends in your strategic foundation document. If only the metrics are there, simply listing what they are is enough for now.

For more on measuring content effectiveness, see *Chapter 10, Measurement.*

## Is your analytics tool integrated with your CMS?

In October 2007, *EContent* magazine published an article by Tony Byrne called, "Mashing Up Web Analytics and Content Management." In it, Byrne writes,

> I know one federal agency that, two years after implementing a web analytics tool, cannot take full advantage of the reports because they can't guarantee that all their pages are tagged, or that they are all tagged properly. And like nearly every other analytics customer, they underestimated the level of effort required to make essential changes to the tags after the initial setup: to account for new categories, new content, and new or improved reports.*

If you're using an analytics tool, either native to or in combination with your CMS, do some research on it. Ask the folks in charge of analytics

---

* www.econtentmag.com/Articles/Editorial/Feature/Mashing-Up-Web-Analytics-and-Content-Management-39578.htm

how the tool works, whether it's working properly, and how its current performance and requirements may have impact on your content recommendations.

### Are you measuring social media?

The larger or more visible your organization, the more likely it is that people are talking about you online via social media channels. What are they saying? Where are they saying it? What is the impact on your business's bottom line? There are multiple methodologies emerging for measuring the ROI of social media, but no silver bullet has emerged. Generally speaking, if measurements are being made and data is available, take it into consideration during your analysis. What you discover may be useful in informing your content strategy.

## WHAT ARE YOUR COMPETITORS UP TO?

Many organizations make the mistake of going to their competitors' websites and freaking out because said competitor has x, y, and z content that *their* website doesn't. Inevitably, there's a fire drill called by someone whose main objectives are to "achieve parity" and "establish competitive advantage" by adding more content to your web properties.

Don't audit and analyze your competitors' websites with the idea that you need to keep up. Consider instead where you can create *true* competitive advantage. Nine times out of ten, this simply means optimizing your current content (in quality and structure); fixing your site search; and beginning to make smart, strategic decisions about which new content you'll add to the site—why, when, how, for whom, by who, and so on.

In order to make strategic recommendations that will set you apart from the crowd, you do need to understand the competitive landscape. When you audit competitor websites, consider the following questions:

## HOW ARE THEIR WEBSITES ORGANIZED?

Redoing your website? By looking at how your competitors structure and label their websites, you will discover:

- Whether industry-standard labels have emerged. For example, if all your competitors are calling their technical support section "Support," you may want to reconsider labeling yours "Tech Experts' Corner."
- If there's a trend towards organizing similar websites by audience, by target market, or by product or service type.
- Where you may be able to borrow (read: steal) intuitive, efficient taxonomies from websites that are clearly doing things right.

## WHICH TOPICS ARE COVERED?

What are your competitors talking about? Again, this is not an exercise to determine what content you're missing. Your web content doesn't need to reach "critical content mass" by including every topic that every competitor includes. Instead, use this as an opportunity to identify where you can create differentiation. What *aren't* your competitors covering? What does your user research demonstrate is most important?

## WHICH CONTENT FORMATS ARE AVAILABLE?

Are your competitors featuring mostly text, or do they have podcasts and video? Do they prefer FAQs or contextual help? Is there a community forum or a review system where user-generated content is helping to inform other people's buying decisions? Are their employees blogging?

See how other organizations are supporting the customer life cycle with their web content types. Identify which options might be well suited to your target audiences, timeframe, internal resources, and budget.

## WHAT'S THEIR BRAND AND MESSAGING LIKE?

You don't want to sound like all the other guys. In fact, you may find that all the other guys sound too marketing-y, too academic, or too technical; this provides you with a tremendous opportunity to stand apart from the crowd by creating content that is conversational and well-structured on the page.

Note things like key messaging (which you don't want to replicate), voice and tone, images, video production values, and so on. What are the brand attributes you'd assign? Is the site's personality consistent page-to-page, or is it all over the map? And so on.

## WHERE ELSE ARE THEY ON THE WEB?

Try to find out what other web content initiatives your competitors have underway. Are they delivering sponsored or branded content on other websites or via social media channels? Have they launched content-driven advertising campaigns? Are there websites that have their own brand identity but are really owned by your competitors? (For example, Johnson & Johnson owns BabyCenter.com.)

## WHO ELSE INFLUENCES YOUR USERS' OPINIONS?

What's more powerful than a website? Faster than an RSS feed? Leaps over your advertising tactics with a single bound? It's the "influencers": people and resources whose opinions inform and shape your customers' opinions of your organization.

In 2008, public relations agency Edelman released its ninth annual "Trust Barometer" survey results. One of their key findings was that, more than ever, people rely on multiple sources of information to form opinions about companies. In fact, from a list of 15 informational resources (including everything from business magazines to blogs to television talk shows), U.S. survey participants ages 25–34 chose Wikipedia (!!) as the second most credible source of information about companies.

What are your customers' top influencers saying about you? Does your web content support, contradict, or include influencer content? Why? Why not?

Here are other influencers to consider. They may not all be relevant to your organization's products or services, but it's worthwhile to check out the ones that are:

- Trade journals and industry associations.
- Analyst reports.
- News media coverage and business magazines (online and offline).
- Television news and talk shows.
- Online message boards and forums.
- Consumer watch groups.
- Bloggers and social media sites.

- Social media recommendations sites (such as Angie's List, Guidestar, or del.icio.us).
- Celebrity speakers or figureheads.
- Friends and family.

## DO CURRENT EVENTS AFFECT YOUR PROJECT?

Everything from the current economy to swiftly-changing governmental regulations can impact your final content recommendations. Some other examples to consider are:

- Political change
- National security
- Environmental concerns
- Technology or scientific advances

How might these current events considerations have impact on a health-care organization? An automobile maker? A manufacturer of airport security devices? A luxury goods retailer? A pharmaceutical company? Spend time considering if and how current events might shape your content strategy and ongoing content maintenance needs.

## AND NOW, IT'S TIME TO MOVE ON.

Congratulations. You've reached the end of your analysis phase.

Maybe it took three days. Maybe it took six months. Regardless, at some point, you have to stop asking questions and start deciding what you want to do with all that information.

Armed with documentation and a clear understanding of exactly where things are today, you're ready to make smart recommendations about any web content that will be included in your web project or long-term initiative.

That's your content strategy. And the time has come to deliver it.

(*Side note:* After all this, can you *believe* people are always waiting until the last minute to figure out their content? Seriously. Blows my mind.)

# 6 STRATEGY

IN CHAPTER 3, DISCIPLINE, you learned the real meaning of the word "strategy": a holistic, well-considered plan for obtaining a specific result.

If a strategy is a road map to get you from where you are to where you want to be, before you can make that plan, you need to understand exactly where you are now. The last chapter showed you how to analyze your current content landscape and ecosystems. Because of your hard work, you're ready to create an achievable, actionable plan to make your wildest content dreams come true.

It's time to create a content strategy.

## YOUR CONTENT STRATEGY = INFORMED RECOMMENDATIONS

Your content strategy documents recommendations about how to create, deliver, and govern web content.

Of course, when it comes to *signing off* on these recommendations, you may not be the "decider" in the end. But after your awesome analysis efforts and after preparing your terrific documentation, you're in a position to put some serious teeth into your content strategy.

To be effective, actionable, and create measurable results, a content strategy must tell us:

- What content do we need, and why?
- How will the content be structured?
- How will users find your web content?
- How we will get from today to launch?
- What's next once the content is "out there?"
- How do these recommendations impact our business?

**These decisions *must* take place during the definition phase of any web project.** As I've said repeatedly, waiting until the creative phase of the project to consider these questions causes pain and suffering all around.

When it comes to deciding what content we need, there's usually a lot of stakeholder brainstorming and project team order-taking. This time, though, you have in-depth analysis that will directly inform (and back up) your content recommendations.

# BEGIN WITH BRAND AND MESSAGING

In the analysis phase, you worked with your organization's brand strategists (or owner) to clearly define brand characteristics and messaging that would inform your content strategy. Now it's time to make recommendations about how brand and messaging will act as the foundation upon which your content strategy will be built.

Your content strategy should define the ways your web content will *demonstrate* your organization-wide brand strategy. This isn't about the talk. It's about how you'll walk the walk.

## BRAND: BROUGHT TO LIFE BY CONTENT

Incorporating your brand into your content strategy doesn't mean finding a bunch of places to stick your brand promise. You can't just tell the reader, "We are seriously committed to x, y, and z." Nobody cares.

If you're a pizza delivery company and you've promised "Fresh, fast delivery!" in all your television commercials, you'd better deliver fresh pizza, fast. Ordering online should be fast and easy, too.

If you're a financial services company that promises to make long-term financial planning easy, are you burying the user in hundreds of pages of how-to articles, overwritten market analyses, and 15-minute videos? Let's hope not.

**Make sure your content recommendations are geared toward demonstrating your brand, not just talking about it.**

## Demonstrate voice and tone

Although it's nothing most readers would notice, your content's brand voice (or "personality") helps users identify whether they like you, understand you, and ultimately trust you.

Your web content might use your corporate brand voice or it might not. For example, a large health care organization may use an uber-professional, corporate brand voice when addressing health care professionals, investors, and the press. But the voice they use for their consumer-facing content should be much more conversational, approachable, and direct.

To introduce the voice and tone qualities you're recommending, a good approach is to offer contrasting values. For example:

- Professional, not academic.
- Confident, not arrogant.
- Clever, not cutesy.
- Savvy, not hipster.
- Expert, not preachy.

Also, when making your recommendations it helps to clearly demonstrate what you're talking about with examples. If you only recommend that the voice should be "authentic, conversational, and inspirational," you're leaving all sorts of room for interpretation. What's "authentic" to you might come off as "trying too hard to be cool" to your readers, for example.

I like to use the "this/not this" as an approach to showing—not just telling—how voice and tone should inform textual content. For example:

| LESS LIKE... | MORE LIKE... |
| --- | --- |
| Contact us. | Get in touch! |
| Our web content offers benefits that go beyond the expected outcome. | More than good web writing. Way more. |
| Our web writing experts have a myriad of creative skills as well as substantial technical expertise in the area of web content. | Our web writers aren't just well-trained. They're seriously talented. |
| At Brain Traffic, we have an enthusiasm and passion for content that shows in everything we do. | Everyone at Brain Traffic loves content. A lot. |

This sort of example is also really helpful for easy knowledge transfer when pulling in writers from other areas to support your primary content creators.

## Recommend style guidelines

Beyond brand values, you'll want to create editorial guidelines that help ensure content consistency and accuracy.

**The style guide, or a specific plan to create the style guide, must be delivered with your content strategy.** Here are some examples of the types of information you may want to include in your style guide or style guide requirements:

- **Brand values.** See the "Brand: How do your users think of you?" section in *Chapter 5, Analysis.*

- **Voice and tone guidelines.** See the "Demonstrate voice and tone" section earlier in this chapter.

- **Correct word usage.** This will vary among organizations. Where various words with the same meaning have been in general use, I recommend choosing one and staying consistent (such as "team member" versus "employee").

- **Product trademark usage.**

- **Web writing considerations.** Specifically, recommend how text links, labeling, metadata, and other repeating content elements should be documented so that they remain consistent throughout your content.

- **Organization's choice of global style guide.** Rather than copying an entire grammar and usage manual into your content style guide, simply refer to the global style guide your organization decides upon, such as the AP manual or the *Chicago Manual of Style*.

- **Web writing best practices.** This information may be a quick, one-page summary of tips on writing web content. For resources on web writing best practices, see the "Web Writing Resources" section in *Chapter 8, Writing*.

It's essential to ensure that the people who are creating, reviewing, and approving your content are all referring to the same playbook. You don't want to leave style open to individual interpretations.

## MESSAGING: DRIVES STORY AND STRUCTURE

During the analysis phase, you collected all of your messages—the pieces of information you want the user to learn or the user wants to see. In the content strategy phase, you make recommendations about how the messages all work together to form useful, usable, enjoyable web content.

### Map your messages to your business objectives and user goals

First, take stock of your messages by ensuring each one helps you achieve at least one of your business objectives or user goals. What is the message helping your content achieve?

If the message doesn't map to any objectives, throw it out. If it maps to a single objective, it's probably a keeper. If it maps to *several* objectives, you've got a real winner.

### Create a message hierarchy

Web content can contain thousands of messages. The key to making these messages valuable and understandable to your user is putting these messages in a hierarchy, like so:

- **Primary message.** The single most important thing you want the user to learn. (This message supports all of your business objectives.)

- **Secondary messages.** A group of key messages that extrapolate the primary message; secondary messages are not ranked, but vary in importance by audience. (Usually maps to several business goals.)
- **Details.** All the facts, data, anecdotes, and philosophies that prove your messages.
- **Call(s) to action.** What you want users to do after they "get" your messages.

When you put all of these messages together, you've got a story.

Think of a magazine article about a business. The primary message is the title. The secondary messages are the subheads, the details are all the sentences between the subheads, and the call to action is the contact information for the business in the sidebar.

When it comes to web content, the story's a lot more complicated. You'll have one major story and many, many subplots all linking to each other. Still, by identifying your main "stories," you'll have an easier time seeing the content that supports, enhances, or expands on those stories as part of the narrative, not just stuff you can tack onto a section of a website.

### Don't forget: Messaging is not content

You don't have to spend days wordsmithing and agonizing over the exact phrasing and wording of messages. Just capture the general idea. Why? Because specific messages are rarely shown to users. Messages aren't content. They're used to select and shape content. So, as you create your content for each page or component, you'll interpret the messages for the audience and page context.

## WHAT CONTENT DO YOU NEED, AND WHY?

If you have current web content online, your content strategy may be about creating content around existing features and functionality. When it comes to a new web initiative, you may have the opportunity to help define what content, features, and functionality should be included. Also, if you're going to be delivering your web content through several different online channels, you may need to identify how that content will be the same (or different) across those channels.

No matter what, thanks to your content analysis, you now have the information you need to make smart decisions.

## RECOMMEND CONTENT THAT MAPS BACK TO YOUR MESSAGES

When you have your primary and secondary messages defined, they're a great way to judge whether proposed content is appropriate for your project.

**Your messages were generated from your business objectives and user needs.** If any recommended content can't be associated with a primary or secondary message, you probably shouldn't recommend it.

If you sell shoes, your primary message may be "we sell quality footwear." So product descriptions, e-commerce features, and information about your manufacturing practices are in. A little widget that shows your local weather forecast on the home page? Not so much. Bye-bye, widget.

## REAL-WORLD RESTRICTIONS, NOT BLUE SKY BRAINSTORMING

When choosing which content to recommend, pay close attention to the requirements and restrictions you identified during the analysis phase. You remember those, right? Budget, timeline, technology, the database, legal requirements… the works.

Recommending content for your project isn't just a matter of consolidating all the stakeholder requests and your own Big Ideas. When you find content that promotes your messages *and* fits within the restrictions of the project, you'll know what content goes online and why.

# HOW WILL USERS SEARCH FOR AND FIND YOUR CONTENT?

You can publish content until the cows come home, but if your users can't find it, it's worthless. Sometimes, it's your job to recommend ways in which your content can be structured and written to ensure maximum findability online. Other times, a search engine specialist or metadata strategist will take the lead. Regardless, this information must be considered in the context of your overall content strategy.

## METADATA

On TheCMSMyth.com, Jeff Cram writes:

> The way you organize, store, and categorize information matters. It matters a lot. After all, most organizations (and websites) are in the information services business. It's all about finding ways to more effectively create, share, repurpose, and distribute content. Your ability to accomplish these goals depends entirely on the way content is organized and classified.
>
> ... It's time for metadata to get the respect and attention it deserves.*

I agree. So here's a very high-level look at how to start wrangling your metadata recommendations.

### Metadata for web search and site search engines

This type of metadata—also known as meta tags—is what shows up about your website in web searches (like Google or Yahoo) and in searches on your own site (if you have a search function, that is). Identifying the keywords you'll use in your metadata is one component of search engine optimization strategy.

Here are the meta tags I'd encourage you to consider:

- **Page title tag** should be the actual title of the page. This is what shows up in Google results in big blue font.

- **Page description tag** describes what's on the page.

- **HTML tags** describe your page headings. (These are very important to web search engines.)

- **Keyword tags** contain the words and phrases you've identified as important to help people find the page during searches, both on the web and on your website.

---

*www.cmsmyth.com/blogs/cms_myth/archive/2009/03/15/why-meta-data-matters.aspx

### Metadata for content management systems

In her book, *Managing Enterprise Content: A Unified Content Strategy,* Ann Rockley addresses the importance of analyzing and designing metadata at the enterprise level:

> In a unified content [management] strategy, metadata enables content to be retrieved, tracked, and assembled automatically. Metadata enables:
>
> - Effective retrieval
> - Systematic reuse
> - Automatic routing based on workflow status
> - Tracking of status
> - Reporting*

If your CMS metadata is inconsistent or poorly managed, your content's going to pile up, and information will be buried. You'll also end up creating redundant content, waste money on inefficient workflow, and generally rack up unnecessary content-related expenses and headaches.

Rockley's book explains how to avoid all that. Bob Boiko also provides stellar guidance on this topic in *The Content Management Bible,* Chapter 24, Working with Metadata.

# GIVING CONTENT FORM AND FUNCTION

For your web content to be findable and usable, it must be structured in ways that are both meaningful and intuitive to your users. And it's the content strategist's responsibility to make recommendations about content structure and design that will support these outcomes.

## HEY, WAIT A MINUTE. ISN'T THIS AN IA'S JOB?

Figuring out how your web content is organized or structured might sound like a job for an information architect (IA). And sometimes, it is.

For small projects, the content strategist may assume information architecture responsibilities, or vice versa. **For larger, content-rich projects, it's preferable to team up a content strategist and an IA.** Together, they'll

---

* Ann Rockley, *Managing Enterprise Content: A Unified Content Strategy,* p. 185.

collaborate on information structure and content design. They may also partner to make evaluations between vendor content management system tools, help to implement the tools, and work to configure the system for the organization's needs.

## IT DOESN'T MATTER. SOMEONE NEEDS TO GET IT DONE.

Whether it's an IA, a content strategist, or both, these are the three levels of content structure and design that need to be recommended:

- Overall content structure.
- Page templates or patterns.
- Page-level requirements.

And no matter which level of content structure you're working on, you'll also need to make recommendations about these content elements:

- Content format.
- Nomenclature (menu labeling).
- Linking strategy.
- CMS content types.
- Related content channels.

One important consideration: **If you're doing a content strategy, and the information architecture is being done by someone else, you still have work to do.** IAs usually focus on structure and functionality, while content strategists focus on the overall story and page-by-page content details. If you own the content, you'll need to be a part of all IA documentation review to ensure that it meets content requirements. In your content strategy documentation, fill in the gaps or make suggestions for change where necessary.

Let's take a closer look at where content strategy and information architecture intersect.

## OVERALL CONTENT STRUCTURE: SITE MAPS

How will your website or other web content be structured? How does the navigation work? What pages live where? What content goes where, or on what page? How do things link together? What elements are on every page of the website?

Recommending and aligning on overall content structure is so important to any web project's success that some of web development's most recognized documentation tools were developed specifically for this purpose:

- **Site map.** Shows the recommended hierarchy of information.
- **Process flows.** Demonstrate how users will move throughout the site or transaction.

These are useful tools, no doubt. But surprisingly, they often fail to document content requirements—even high-level ones.

Take, for example the page stack. When an information architect (or user experience designer) doesn't have time (or tools, or skill set, or motivation) to document content requirements, they stick a "page stack" on their site map.

Here's what it looks like:

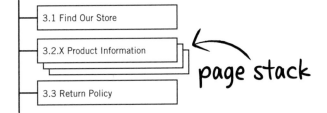

In his book *Don't Make Me Think*, Steve Krug describes page stacks as a smoke-and-mirrors way of abdicating responsibility for what actually happens after the first few levels of navigation. Krug says that, with page stacks, the IA is basically telling project stakeholders, "… and then the MAGIC happens!"

Page stacks are fine if the site map comes part-and-parcel with detailed recommendations about content. If it doesn't, the content owners are stuck with no direction, no context, and no idea what should actually go on those magically stacked pages.

The collaboration between an IA and a content strategist ensures that the content is being considered not just as a collection of elements that require order, but also as actual content that requires planning, editorial oversight, and care and feeding over time.

## PAGE TEMPLATES: FINDING PATTERNS IN CONTENT STRUCTURE

In general, websites are more user-friendly when they're consistent: in brand, in visual design, in content voice and tone, and in structure. Providing users with consistency gives them a sense of confidence that they'll be able to find what they came looking for. They maintain a "sense of place" no matter where they are on your site. And they definitely won't feel that they're visiting fourteen different websites instead of one.

Because of this, as well as to make visual design and content management more streamlined, IAs often create "page templates"—wireframes or diagrams that represent page-level content that repeats throughout your website.

These templates—which often look pretty much like wireframes—are generally focused on page layout and functional requirements. The navigation goes here. The search box goes here.

But when it comes to demonstrating where content goes on the page, the IA will usually draw a box and either leave it empty or fill it up with "greek text" (also known as "lorem ipsum"). This looks great to everyone in usability testing and during visual design. But when it comes time to fill up those boxes with real content, things often fall apart.

Enter the content strategist, who works with the IA to help define actual content requirements for each template.

As part of that process, the content strategist needs to prove that the IA's templates are actionable. Because, guess what? When you start putting real text into those templates? Turns out that much of the time, that page template isn't going to work for much of the content you designed it for.

## PAGE-LEVEL REQUIREMENTS: MAKING CONTENT RECOMMENDATIONS REAL

In most IA documentation, page- (or component-) level content requirements are captured in wireframes, which are similar to architectural
blueprints. Or, if you're lucky, the IA may also build a prototype of the IA
recommendations, which is a functioning version of a few pages of your
website or web content components.

These tools, when used effectively, can very accurately document content
requirements for the pages they show. But there are a few problems with
them, too.

First, typical IA wireframes and prototypes show only a few "representa-
tive" pages of the website. (Obviously, it wouldn't be cost- or time-efficient
to do them for every page.)

Second, there's some seriously important information about the content
itself that's missing: consideration of (or input on) key messages, specific
content recommendations, source content quality, and requirements for
how to create and maintain the content.

To close the gap, we need to introduce a new layer of "design," which consid-
ers how content—defined and driven by messaging, business objectives, and
user goals—will receive the attention it deserves, at the right time in the
project process.

### Introducing page tables

In order to take site maps and page templates to the next level, the level at
which key content recommendations may be identified and explained, we
need a third type of documentation. This document is called a *page table*.

Page tables were first introduced in 2003 by Melissa Rach (Brain Traffic).
The page table tells you everything you need to know about the content on
a specific website page (or content module)—from the objective and source
content to the content recommendations and their implications, including
requirements for creation, delivery, and maintenance.

Here's a simple version:

Page tables are done in Microsoft Word and can be created far more quickly than wireframes and prototypes. It's also easy for stakeholders to edit and change, which is critical when there are tons of pages to review.

## When page tables aren't enough... or too much

On a website with hundreds, thousands, or hundreds or thousands of pages, it's neither cost-effective nor time-efficient to create a page table for every single piece of content. Sites of this magnitude include:

- **E-commerce sites:** Mostly product descriptions.

- **Encyclopedic sites:** Sites that offer thousands of articles indexed by topic.

- **News sites:** Articles and other content artifacts (images, audio, video) that are typically archived both by date and topic.

In these cases, you can create a content requirements template (formatted like a page table) for all pages that have the *exact* same purpose and use. Not "sort of similar" pages or components. *Exactly* similar, like a press release, a product description, or a specific type of article.

**Regardless of website size, all content recommendations need to *somehow* be documented to assist with content creation, maintenance, and migration tasks.**

On a really big website, you may want to get a report from the CMS to keep track of all of the content with the same page type. On a mid-sized website (200 to 1,200 pages), it may be more helpful to create a large spreadsheet to keep track of the content that fits into your content requirements template. (It depends on your CMS and your technical abilities.)

Whatever your content considerations, without some form of documentation—what you have, what you need, and why—you're stuck with a big dumping ground of content that's likely to fall prey to irrelevance, inaccuracy, and inconsistency. Keep up with what you have.

## STRUCTURAL SUPPORT: PROVIDING CONTEXT FOR YOUR CONTENT

Now that you have an idea of your content universe and how users will navigate their way through it, you need to make recommendations about their moment-to-moment experience of and interaction with your content. How can you best provide context, not only for their unique goals (gathering information, completing tasks, communicating, and so on) but also for your content itself?

To ensure your content strategy is comprehensive, here are the recommendations you'll need to include about content structure.

### Nomenclature (also known as labeling)

Information architects are often expected to identify which labels will be assigned to different sections of a website. This task applies not only to navigational menus but also content modules (for example, my favorite overused and meaningless label, "Related Links").

By collaborating with a word-savvy, message-focused content strategist, the IA has a partner who will:

- Keep an eye on how labels might support key messages.
- Collaborate closely to ensure context, consistency, and clarity at every level of required labeling.
- Above all else, ensure that the labels are intuitive to end users.

## Content formats

Content format is the medium in which your content will be delivered online: text, audio, visual, video, animation, infographics, and so on.

The content strategist should always work closely with the user experience design team to develop recommendations for content formats. On the flip side, user experience designers shouldn't make decisions about content formats without requesting input from a content strategist. It's pointless to design a user experience without a deep understanding of the content that will fuel that experience.

When recommending content formats, consider:

- **How can you best demonstrate your key messages?** For example, if you're a tool manufacturer, and you target the home do-it-yourself market, you may want to invest in a series of how-to articles focusing on home projects. It also might be smart to produce a video series showing how to do those same projects step-by-step.
- **Are these formats achievable?** It's easy to brainstorm great ideas, but they're useless unless they're workable. Do you have the time and resources to create a video series? If you decide on a weekly podcast, can you commit the time to prepare for the podcast, record, edit, and publish it?
- **How "portable" will your content be?** Users love to share content— they link to it, email it, embed it in their blogs. Will your content formats encourage or discourage this sharing? Are you comfortable letting your content "be free," or are there copyright or legal considerations that prohibit it?

## Linking strategy

When you make recommendations for a linking strategy, you're recommending how and when certain links will appear in the content or navigation that will work to support business objectives and user goals. For example, your linking strategy can plan to:

- Drive users to tasks that support fulfillment of business objectives.
- Steer users towards additional, related information that may support their decision-making processes.
- Offer relevant pieces of information that will further engage the user in your brand experience.
- Encourage users to join an online community, participate in a social media channel, or comment on a blog.

Be sure to call out where links should appear, under which circumstances they should appear, how they should be written, and any consistent calls to action.

## CMS content types

If you're looking at creating content that will be stored in and delivered by a CMS, one key requirement of a content strategy is to map, define, and label your content types. For example, a content type might define:

- The document template that the content will be based on.
- Metadata the content will have associated with it.
- Workflows that the content will use.
- Information management policies that apply to the content.

It's likely that this section of your content strategy document will only be a summary of a much more complex, comprehensive content model. For a detailed explanation of the relationship between content components, types, and elements, please see Chapter 27 of Bob Boiko's *The Content Management Bible.*

## Content channels

How will content be distributed to the user? Assumedly via the web, but will it only be available on your website? How about mobile, RSS feed, email, online press releases, blogs, or participation in social media?

The two primary considerations here are *where* your audiences are, and *how* they want to receive (or pull) content from your organization. Of course, the delivery channels available in your organization, as well as the resources you have available to create and maintain that content, will also have impact on your recommendations.

**The more places you deliver content, and the more people you have involved with the creation and delivery of that content, the more important it is to have a cohesive content strategy in place to ensure consistency across channels.** While this is an obvious consideration for traditional marketing campaigns, it's often more difficult to achieve with online channels, especially given the immediacy with which content can be delivered.

# DOCUMENTING CONTENT REQUIREMENTS AND SOURCES

At this point in your content strategy recommendations, it's time to put together an actionable plan about how those recommendations will actually be implemented. Without a real-world plan, any strategy is pretty much just a pile of useless documentation that's full of a bunch of "good ideas."

The good news is that you collected all the information you need to inform this plan of action in the analysis phase. Resources, timeline, budget, and source content are all carefully documented. It's now up to you to figure out how to make the content happen.

## CONTENT REQUIREMENTS: WHERE THE RUBBER HITS THE ROAD

Once the content structure and information architecture process is complete, either the IA or the content strategist needs to actually pull together a spreadsheet of new content requirements.

The format of this list looks a lot like the content inventory you completed during your content audit (see *Chapter 4, Audit*). For your new content requirements spreadsheet, however, you're specifically listing out *every single page or content component* that needs to be created.

(Similarly, if you're preparing for a content migration process from one server or CMS to another, you need to identify what's getting moved, and where. Different kind of requirements, same output.)

In general, the resulting document is merely a useful, "snapshot" summary of the detailed recommendations you provided in the page tables. The two necessary columns are the page (or component) ID, which should match up with the site map; and the page (or component) title, which should be unique.

Beyond these two fields, the content requirements spreadsheet can be used to document a variety of content-related considerations during the creation process, including:

- Content owners (creators, reviewers, approvers)
- Source content location
- Missing source content
- Document versions
- Open questions
- Metadata requirements
- SEO keywords (mapped per page)
- CMS attribute requirements
- … and so on

The content strategist or lead web editor should be in charge of keeping this document fully up-to-date, because it serves as the primary reference for all content owners during the creation process. It can also be an extraordinarily useful artifact post-launch in helping to track content maintenance requirements or to scope future qualitative audits.

## SOURCE CONTENT: WHERE'S THIS ALL GOING TO COME FROM?

Now that you've identified which content needs to be created, your content strategy needs to define where that content will come from.

The good news is, there are several options for acquiring content to fulfill your content strategy. The bad news is, there's no truly easy way to "get content." Even if you buy ready-made content, editorial oversight is still required to ensure that co-created or third-party content meets your organization's brand guidelines, web standards, and user needs.

Let's look at the pros and cons of each option.

## Original content

Content created by and for your unique organization is by far the most valuable kind of content. It's also the most expensive. But when you take the time to really understand your audiences; create content specifically for and about them, in a voice that's uniquely yours; then deliver your content in formats that engage and motivate; you're delivering the kind of user experience that will bring people back for more.

To create original content, you need source material and ideas. During the analysis phase, you (hopefully) collected all of the possible source content that is available. In addition, you will likely need to interview subject matter experts and do your own research.

## Aggregated content

There are two ways to go about aggregating web content.

The first is to automatically aggregate content from other websites or sources. This can be accomplished in several ways. For example, you can pull content with an RSS feed, which pulls content from the websites or feeds you subscribe to. You could also create search algorithms, which pull content based on specific keywords or phrases.

The primary risk, here, is that content is being published or linked to from your organization without any sort of qualitative review. The tools provide a filter of sorts, bringing in content they calculate to be of some worth. However, you're also making a big assumption that, based on subscription choices and keywords, that content will have relevancy and context for your audience. And that's a risk, too.

The second way to aggregate content is to have someone curate it. This means a select person or team of people is actively searching for content that meets unique standards identified by the content strategist. In my opinion, content curation offers tremendous value to your users. On the product side, MightyGoods.com and CoolHunting.com have found huge success simply by shopping around the web, identifying unique and extraordinary products (or sometimes, deals), and sharing their findings online. Bloggers or Twitter users who regularly find and link to content they know their audiences will appreciate are rewarded by repeat visits and subscribers. **In a world of information overload, content curation is a valuable service that can be offered by any organization with a point of view, be it product-focused, service-oriented, or other.**

Please note that content curation is *not* the same as asking users to provide content reviews or ratings. Simply asking your users to rate your web content does not ensure that the most relevant, valuable content will be surfaced. Ratings can be seriously skewed by just a few active (and opinionated) users.

## Co-created content

Big brands are making the most of high-profile bloggers, studios, podcasters, and other entities who are already in the business of creating content for an engaged audience or subscriber base. And that's smart.

If you're a food company, consider reaching out to popular food bloggers and hiring them to blog for your brand, either on your website or another sponsored channel. If you're a city or state visitors' bureau, identify local photographers who will regularly upload photos to an online photo album featuring the best of your area. While you do give up some control of the content being generated with this approach, you're gaining built-in audiences, unique perspectives that can complement your brand strategies, and the opportunity to experiment with a wide range of content types, often for less time and money than would otherwise be involved.

## Licensed content

If your content strategy includes offering a deeper library of online resources than you have the infrastructure to create, the content strategist may recommend licensing content created by a third-party publisher. (In this instance, it would also be the content strategist's responsibility to research, review, and recommend third-party content providers.)

Articles, images, audio, and video are all widely available for licensing online. Again, you may be risking brand dilution by offering generic content to your online users. However, this is a hugely popular (albeit questionably successful) option for a wide range of industry websites. For example, health insurers license content from WebMd, Staywell, the Harvard Medical School, and more.

Don't forget that licensed content still requires research and oversight.

### User-generated content

Another way to source content for your web properties is to invite users to create it, themselves.

This is a fairly complicated, surprisingly resource-intensive approach to sourcing content. If you build a user-generated content forum, it doesn't necessarily mean that they will come. And if they do come, it doesn't mean they'll stick around. **Engagement tactics are key, as are resources that will moderate and respond to content and comments.**

Social media strategies invite users to participate with your branded content in ways you may plan for, but also (and inevitably) in ways you can't possibly anticipate. For example, an SUV manufacturer recently invited their users to co-create commercials promoting a new SUV model. The campaign backfired when environmentalists stormed the virtual gates, creating commercials that damned SUVs as gas-guzzling, nature-killing, road-hogging beasts.

No matter what the social media "experts" say, don't just dive in to user-generated content tactics. Plan, test, measure, respond. Just because it works beautifully for some brands doesn't mean it will for yours. Proceed with caution.

## GETTING FROM RECOMMENDATIONS TO LAUNCH

One of the content strategist's most valuable contributions to any project is the content creation plan.

This plan details:

- Which content needs to be created.
- Who is responsible for each and every piece of content.
- How the source content maps to new content requirements.

- Where the content will be stored and delivered throughout the creation process.
- How the content will get done on time and on budget.

By solving these problems in the definition phase of any project, we're able to ensure that all our recommendations about what content to create and deliver are actually achievable, thereby avoiding project implosion when it comes time to "go get the content." All of this information should be *as detailed as possible* in the content strategy document, or in the accompanying documentation.

## SCHEDULE: THESE THINGS TAKE TIME

The analysis you did early in the project should provide you with the real-world information you need to make recommendations about the content creation and publication schedule. Factors to consider include resources, skill sets, number of reviewers, and so on.

When outlining the initial content schedule proposal, consider:

- Has the amount of content changed from the statement of work?
- Is the amount of content doable within resource constraints (including time, budget, and people power)?
- How much time is required for the various types of approval?
- When can the development team begin accepting final content for production? Can the deliverables be staggered?

### Don't let the project manager guess about the content schedule

I love project managers. Deeply. But they don't often have a grasp on how long web content really takes to complete.

I recently had a partner agency call in a panic. They were working on a large website due to launch in less than four weeks, and their team of three copywriters were seriously behind with their deliverables. Apparently, the project manager had looked at the content requirements (about 600 pages, give or take), assumed three writers could finish 200 pages each over an eight-week period (25 pages a week? No problem!), and kicked things off with high expectations.

Six weeks later, the writers had completed 115 pages between them. That meant there were 485 pages due in two weeks, or ten business days.

I ran the numbers and informed her that, at the rate her writers were going, she would need to pull in an additional 15 full-time writers the next day, give them four hours of ramp-up time, then have them working round-the-clock to meet the deadline.

Not surprisingly, the project launch was moved back a few months.

### Don't forget translation and localization

If you have translation and localization requirements, be sure to budget plenty of extra time. It's not enough simply to translate from one language to another. You also need to ensure that the translation takes into account cultural, linguistic, and stylistic differences between countries and regions. Furthermore, graphics and callouts need to be considered, as one image may mean something completely different in another country.

Plan realistically for the time and resources translation and localization will require. Consider who will be responsible, and how translated content will be governed both at the enterprise level and locally.

## WHAT HAPPENS TO THE CONTENT AFTER LAUNCH?

If you're not careful, your web content may quickly become outdated, inaccurate, or irrelevant to your audiences. So you need to ask the question: what's going to happen to it once it's "out there"?

We'll dig a bit deeper into the how and why of content governance in *Chapter 11, Maintenance.* But here are the primary questions that should be answered in the content strategy document:

- If you have a future release planned in the near term (within a year), what content will be on it (high-level)?
- How do you know when to make changes? Or, how to set rules for content updates?
- What kind of maintenance does your content need?
- Who is going to take care of your content?

Many of the answers to these questions can be captured in a web editorial calendar.

If you can, articulate your case for the utility of such a calendar. Even a simple spreadsheet that pulls together various communications plans will shed light on what's being published or released when, where it's happening, and whether or not the web team needs to plan for its impact on content.

## HOW DO THESE RECOMMENDATIONS IMPACT OUR BUSINESS?

This is an often-overlooked but incredibly important topic to address in the context of your content strategy recommendations.

Sometimes, your recommendations will have a specific impact on parts or all of your organization. Content maintenance requires people to assume responsibility for it. Licensing third-party content requires a budget. Both short- and long-term ramifications may need to be considered for stakeholders to make smart decisions about your recommendations.

Other examples of content strategy recommendations that may impact your organization include:

- **Brand and messaging.** How does this information need to play out in other communications materials, online and offline?
- **Scope.** Do you need a bigger budget? More resources during creation and maintenance phases?
- **Changing workflow and responsibilities.** How will these recommendations affect current staffing and processes?
- **Changes to databases and other technology.** What are the cost and resource impacts? How will content publication and delivery be affected?
- **New topics or reworked content.** For example, how will updates to a product section change the questions customers may ask when they call your service department?

- **User-generated or social media content.** Who should be responsible? How will negative reactions from users be managed? How will voice and tone be implemented and overseen?

- **Required collaboration or alignments.** How will SEO, marketing, public relations, and other roles need to be informed and included in the content creation and maintenance phases?

**People need to be well-prepared for these business impacts before content strategy recommendations are implemented.** Make sure documentation is clear and easy to understand. You'll need alignment from key stakeholders, and possibly from other folks who will be affected by any business impact. Communicate the benefits. Make them feel like they're part of the team.

Remember, a big part of strategy is getting people on your side. Everybody talks about getting user input and buy-in—but make sure your business stakeholders are given the opportunity to weigh in, too, and make *absolutely* sure they're aligned on your recommendations.

## NOW YOU'VE DONE IT.

So. Here we are.

You've done a deep dive analysis of your content and all the factors that have a significant impact on future content creation, delivery, and maintenance.

You've made informed, achievable recommendations about how to create, deliver, and govern the content.

You've taken responsibility for defining and designing detailed content recommendations at every step of the user experience, helping your users find information and complete tasks with more efficiency and enjoyment than ever.

You've defined real-time, real-world content requirements and set up a tool that will support a streamlined content creation process, help manage deadlines and scope, and keep everyone on the same page.

And now?

*Now* you are ready to start the content creation process.

# CREATE

Content on the web is a living, breathing thing. It's ever-changing, ever-evolving, constantly shaped and reshaped by curators, creators, reviewers, and users. Prepare your content carefully, and it will live a longer, happier life online.

# 7  WORKFLOW

AS ANNE CABORN, principal of Content Delivery & Analysis in London, likes to say, "Content doesn't just happen."

If the content creation and maintenance process doesn't seem overwhelming to you, you're probably missing a few steps. Analyze. Synthesize. Create. Review. Edit. Review again. Approve. Publish. Maintain. Repeat. Repeat. Repeat.

Luckily, there's a way to tame the beast: Workflow.

## WORKFLOW IS WORTH IT

As you know, many people seriously underestimate how long it takes to create content. This creates bottlenecks and heartache for project stakeholders, and often delays launch or content delivery significantly.

By including a content workflow in your content strategy, you can be assured that critical roles are filled, responsibilities are understood, and timelines are actually achievable.

In this chapter we'll examine workflow in depth. We'll consider:

- What is workflow?
- How do you design a workflow?
- How do you get people to adopt a new workflow?

## SO, WHAT'S A WORKFLOW?

The content workflow defines how content is requested, sourced, created, reviewed, approved, and delivered.

A content workflow is designed with the following three focus areas in mind:

- **Process.** From start to finish, how does content travel through your organization and onto the web?

- **Tasks.** Which tasks are required to make the content useful, usable, and enjoyable to your audiences?

- **People.** Who is responsible for ensuring the content is accurate, timely, on brand, contextual, and so forth?

Your content strategy may outline a newly recommended content workflow, or it may simply document a workflow that's already in place. Regardless, **by documenting workflow, you'll have a very clear vision of how, when, and by whom the work will get done.**

*Note:* Content workflow, as discussed in this chapter, is independent of (albeit sometimes related to) content management system requirements and design. In my experience, workflow that's designed based on CMS features does not solve the underlying challenges related to human resource and content governance, which is our focus for this chapter. For more on content workflow as it relates to back-end, technical content management, refer to Bob Boiko's book, *The Content Management Bible,* Chapter 33, Designing Workflow and Staffing Models.

## DESIGNING WORKFLOW

No matter how small your website or organization, having a web content workflow in place helps to ensure that your content is accurate, consistent, and timely.

## UNDERSTAND THE CONTENT CREATION PROCESS

The workflow process encompasses every task and person necessary to deliver your content online.

Richard Sheffield's book *The Web Content Strategist's Bible* is an excellent primer for anyone who is trying to get their organization's web content under control. Sheffield offers these guidelines for designing an effective content workflow for the people responsible for your web content:

1. Determine a starting point for your workflow. (*Author's note:* This could be any kind of content request or requirement, either spontaneous or scheduled.)

2. Figure out a logical place for the workflow to end. (*Author's note:* Some might say this is when content is delivered online; I would argue it shouldn't end until content is archived or destroyed.)

3. Identify all players from beginning to end of the workflow. (*Author's note:* This should include not only content stakeholders but also information architects, designers, developers, and anyone else who may need to weigh in on any content requests.)

4. Sketch the tasks.

5. Identify interaction patterns among players and tasks.

6. Allocate time frames for tasks.

7. Identify notification patterns: who needs to know what at any given stage of the workflow.

8. Identify approval patterns.

9. Determine all the "what ifs" that may knock your workflow off its path.

10. Once all roles are identified, tasks are sketched, and notification and approval patterns are identified, examine your workflow to see if it can be simplified.

Sheffield's approach is straightforward and rooted in common sense. Anyone can tackle this exercise and end up with incredibly useful results.

Here's a very simple example of a content workflow that might result from this exercise:

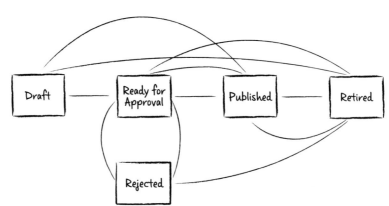

Things start to get interesting when you're dealing with things like distributed publishing (where multiple parties are publishing, possibly across channels and platforms) and interdependent workflows. The larger the organization and the more complex the publishing requirements, the more important it is to have established processes and guidelines for your content lifecycle.

## DIG INTO THE DETAILS

To define an achievable content workflow, you need to figure out exactly what's happening (or not), where it's happening, how it's getting done (or not), and who's in charge (or not). Ideally, this discovery will happen during the research and analysis phase. However, if you're in-house at an organization, it can happen at any time, since assumedly there is always content moving through different stages of development.

Here's a fairly comprehensive list of questions to help you find your way.

### How does content happen?

- How is content being created?
- How are content efforts being planned for and documented?
- How do offline communications efforts inform or link to online content?

- If translation is required, how is it completed? In-house? By freelancers or vendors? Onsite at global locations? How are translations assigned and approved?

- How does content move from desktop programs to the staging server or online environment?

- How are content quality assurance findings tracked and communicated? How are final updates made and approved?

- How are live content errors caught, tracked, and corrected?

- Are there different rules for different kinds of content? (for example, a blog versus a product page)

- How does the process for purchasing or aggregating content differ from in-house content creation?

- How does legal prefer to review content and when?

- How is content ultimately delivered online?

- How is content archived or deleted? Manually, or is it an automated process within the CMS?

## Where does content happen?

- Where do requests for new or updated content come from?

- Where are new requests routed?

- Where is source content (or reusable content, like a component library) stored?

- How are content drafts routed between authors, approvers, and publishers?

- Where is content staged (on a server, online) for review and quality assurance?

- Where does content governance sit within the organization, if anywhere?

- Geographically, where are content owners located? Do time differences or language barriers impact on how and when content is created, approved, published?

## When does content happen?

- Which business drivers (such as product launches, financial quarters, holidays, news, events) trigger requests for new or updated content?

- Are there "emergency" content requests that arise? If so, what are they, why are they considered emergencies, and who can submit them?

- Is there an editorial calendar that details what needs to be delivered online and when? Does the calendar integrate other communications efforts to ensure consistency of information?

- Are there processes in place for on-the-fly updates and changes? When are these possible or acceptable?

- Are there regularly scheduled content updates? How often do they occur?

- Do IT production schedules inform content updates? How and when?

- What is the average time from content request to publish date?

# IDENTIFY YOUR PEOPLE

The most important, dynamic components of your workflow are human beings, those messy creatures whose habits, politics, preferences, and ambitions tend to have impact on, well, everything.

You must clearly understand the individual roles, responsibilities, skill sets, and agendas of the people you'll rely on to get your content done right and on time. Their individual perspectives and pursuits radically inform the measures you'll take when implementing a content workflow.

## Today, who's doing what?

Start your discovery process by asking these questions to anyone and everyone you can:

- Who can request content? Who can approve or deny the request, and on what grounds? Who creates the assignment? These people are your content *requesters*.

- Who is responsible for sourcing existing content or delivering new information that will inform new content creation? These people are your content *providers*.

- Who is responsible for creating new content? Who is responsible for editing source content? These people are your content *creators*.

- Who must review each draft, and for which specific purpose(s)? Who fact checks the work? Who proofs (or copyedits) the content? These people are your content *reviewers*.

- Who has the authority to approve or reject edits? Who is responsible for legal approval? Who is responsible for final approval prior to delivery? These people are your content *approvers*.

- Who moves the content from the desktop or server environment to the web? These people are your content *publishers*.

Once you have them identified, your key players will need to share important information with you about their individual processes or habits. Start with the questions in the sections that follow. These questions overlap with the task identifications above, but they're specific to each type of content owner and will help surface information that will inform process and tasks.

## Ask requesters...

- What are the various instances that trigger a request for content to be published?

- How do you think this content can help us meet business objectives and user needs?

- Have they identified times when a content request should have been initiated but was not? Why?

- Which standards are you using to measure those triggers? For example, low priority, medium priority, immediate priority?

- Who can make requests to publish? Why?

- What do you perceive as your key challenges or obstacles related to web content production and upkeep? Why? How would you like to see things changed?

- Where and when do you provide source material, or are you leaving that up to someone else (*providers*)?

- How would you like to see this content take shape online?

- How do you want or need to participate in the content review and approval processes?

- How do you find out when your request has been fulfilled?

## Ask providers...

- How do you determine if the source content with which you're providing us is on-brand? Accurate? Up-to-date? Approved by legal?

- If we have questions about the source content, who are the subject matter experts we should contact?

## Ask creators...

- How and when would you like to be engaged in a web content project?

- How much time does it typically take to do a first draft (or round of concepts, or rough edit) of [insert content type here]? Explain your process.

- What information is most helpful for you to have before you begin working on the content?

- Who and what do you need access to during the content development process? Do you need to consult or work with IAs, designers, developers, or other web professionals? If so, when and how?

- What are your key challenges or obstacles related to web content creation?

- Who is empowered to accept or reject changes from the reviewers and approvers? Upon what grounds?

- How are you made aware of updates to style guides and legal requirements? How often?

- Which tools do you use (or wish you had) for content creation and updates?

- Are you able to view content in a staging environment, or do you just see the final product? Does the staging environment inform any changes or edits that you're able to make?

## Ask reviewers and approvers...

- How and when would you like to be engaged in a web content project?

- When you review web content, what are your primary objectives?

- How and when would you like to receive content that requires your review or approval?

- Where do you keep an up-to-date style guide available for reference?

### Ask publishers...

- In what format would you like to receive web content to be published?

- How long do you require to publish new content, changes to content, and so on? Explain your process.

- What do you wish we understood about the opportunities and challenges you have with our current publishing technologies?

- Is there a standard workflow for content publication? How is it documented and shared?

- How does our organization view the content life cycle? What are the triggers for current content review, archiving, or removal?

# MAKING IT HAPPEN

Once your content workflow has been identified or designed, you'll need to figure out a smart way to tell people about it and motivate them to adopt the process.

There are a few things to consider here:

### Make people feel included

As you have been working with people throughout your discovery process, you've been asking for their insights and input around content. Hopefully, you've incorporated their feedback into your workflow design. Therefore, they're already somewhat invested in this thing you're doing to make their lives easier. So that's a good start.

### Communicate the benefits

Old habits die hard. Don't expect to send a PDF of the workflow design to your coworkers and have everything running smoothly the next day. People do things the way they like to do them, regardless of whether or not it's the most efficient way. **Figure out how you can introduce the workflow process by clearly communicating the benefits not only to the organization as a whole but to the individuals who will be responsible for making the workflow a success.** If you can sell the idea that this will make everyone's life easier, you'll be more than halfway there.

### Give it time

People will need some time to adapt to a new workflow, especially if you are simultaneously teaching people how to use a new CMS. Identify your success measures. Track usage. Celebrate short-term wins. Make sure people are clearly seeing the end-product benefits: that content is more accurate, more consistent, more in line with their vision of what it should be.

### Oversee the process

**Make sure there's governance for your content workflow.** Without someone overseeing the work stream (or multiple work streams), it's not going to work. Preferably, this person (or team) has some form of editorial oversight, as well as the authority themselves (or through management support) to enforce standards and guidelines. If you put a process-monger in place, who is only looking at requirements and not the end product, the content will be treated like packets being moved down an assembly line. That works with technical features. Not with content.

## BETTER PROCESS MEANS BETTER CONTENT

Establishing a content workflow allows employees to understand where they fit in the larger scheme of content development; how they specifically contribute to the end product; and where the system breaks down if they don't deliver.

Content workflow also ensures that all the right eyes are on the content before it ever gets delivered online. This should ensure better quality and consistency across the board.

**Don't leave content workflow to your CMS.** A technology platform can't tell you if your content is meaningful, accurate, or actionable. Only human beings can do that.

# 8 WRITING

IN CHAPTER 3, we defined content as text, data, graphics, video, and audio. So why am I singling out writing in a book about content strategy?

What I actually want to talk about is the person who's *doing* the writing: The web writer. Here are just a few of the many reasons:

- The majority of the online content that helps our audiences find information and complete tasks is still text.
- Many content strategists take on the role of the web writer on some projects—which can confuse stakeholders about the strategist's primary role.
- Web writers are more directly affected by content strategy than any other web team member.

In the context of content strategy for the web, the role of a web writer merits examination, definition, and defense.

## WEB WRITING: CONTENT STRATEGY IN ACTION

More often than not, it's the web writer's responsibility to turn content strategy recommendations into real content the user sees and appreciates. It's the web writer's work that ultimately produces tangible results any business stakeholder can see and understand.

And so, in this chapter, we'll discuss:

- The difference between copy and content.
- The job of a web writer.
- When to call the web writer.
- More resources about web writing.

## IT'S NOT COPY. IT'S CONTENT.

The role of the web writer is hugely misunderstood by most organizations and web project teams. It's constantly being confused with the role of a copywriter, and it's not. It's more.

I was a web writer before I was a content strategist. And I was a copywriter before that.

As a copywriter, I loved brainstorming creative ideas for advertising campaigns. I took great pleasure in writing and rewriting sentences and paragraphs until they clearly, powerfully communicated exactly what I wanted them to. I wrote sales scripts, product descriptions, catalog copy, annual reports, brochures, headlines, billboards, newspaper ads, the works.

Here's how my copywriting projects usually went down:

1. Someone would identify the need for copy in a design, print piece, television or radio ad, outdoor advertisement, or something similar.
2. They'd call me.
3. I'd go in, sit down, and review the creative or project brief with the project owner. Perhaps this person would provide some source material. I'd get a deadline. We'd shake hands and part.
4. I would go somewhere and write.
5. I would send my copy draft to the project owner. They'd reply with edits. This might happen a few times. Sometimes I'd even work with the designer, which meant I got to see my words come alive with visuals.
6. Finally, the project owner would approve the copy.
7. I would get paid.

This, indeed, is copywriting. Concept. Create. Revise. Approve.

This, however, is content:

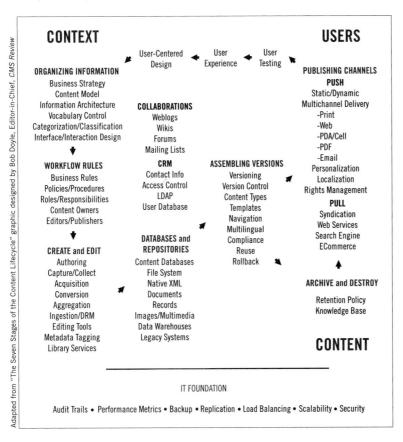

Adapted from "The Seven Stages of the Content Lifecycle" graphic designed by Bob Doyle, Editor-in-Chief, *CMS Review*

**CONTEXT**      **USERS**

User-Centered Design    User Experience    User Testing

**ORGANIZING INFORMATION**
Business Strategy
Content Model
Information Architecture
Vocabulary Control
Categorization/Classification
Interface/Interaction Design

**COLLABORATIONS**
Weblogs
Wikis
Forums
Mailing Lists

**PUBLISHING CHANNELS**
**PUSH**
Static/Dynamic
Multichannel Delivery
-Print
-Web
-PDA/Cell
-PDF
-Email
Personalization
Localization
Rights Management

**WORKFLOW RULES**
Business Rules
Policies/Procedures
Roles/Responsibilities
Content Owners
Editors/Publishers

**CRM**
Contact Info
Access Control
LDAP
User Database

**ASSEMBLING VERSIONS**
Versioning
Version Control
Content Types
Templates
Navigation
Multilingual
Compliance
Reuse
Rollback

**PULL**
Syndication
Web Services
Search Engine
ECommerce

**CREATE and EDIT**
Authoring
Capture/Collect
Acquisition
Conversion
Aggregation
Ingestion/DRM
Editing Tools
Metadata Tagging
Library Services

**DATABASES and REPOSITORIES**
Content Databases
File System
Native XML
Documents
Records
Images/Multimedia
Data Warehouses
Legacy Systems

**ARCHIVE and DESTROY**
Retention Policy
Knowledge Base

**CONTENT**

IT FOUNDATION

Audit Trails • Performance Metrics • Backup • Replication • Load Balancing • Scalability • Security

Usually, when I show this graphic to people, they cringe. Sometimes they even groan out loud. To which I respond, "Welcome to the world of the web writer."

# THE WEB WRITER'S REAL JOB

I'm sure there are many, many copywriters out there who would like to believe that the messy content lifecycle has nothing to do with them. These folks have no desire to live in a world where words like "content inventory" and "metadata" and "nomenclature" are used on a daily basis.

And that's fine. Just don't hire those writers to work on your web content.

To write truly effective web content, a writer needs to care deeply about—and take responsibility for—helping online readers find information and complete tasks.

## THEY HAVE TO BE PROBLEM SOLVERS...

**The web writer's mission? Useful, usable content that's also enjoyable.** It's her job to begin a conversation with the reader that results in mutually beneficial outcomes all around. A problem solved. An article found. A connection made.

These things don't happen with just a well-turned phrase. They happen only when a writer takes the time to:

- Understand why writing for the web is different from writing for print, and how to do it well.
- Attend usability sessions and observe how people behave online.
- Learn the fundamentals of information architecture and user experience design.
- Develop the habit of ongoing, on-the-fly web content analysis (also known as "compulsive editing of other people's work").
- Master the basics of web content search engine optimization.
- Learn to love content inventories, as these documents are the writer's primary reference point for what content is required, when it's due, which source content applies, and other information that's relevant to the writing phase of any content project.
- Take on header tags, search keywords, page structure, messaging hierarchy, text links, error messages, and so on.

For writers, it's a different ball game out there on the interwebs. And it's a game not every writer is willing to learn or train for, let alone play.

## ... AND THEY HAVE TO WRITE WELL, TOO

Put aside all of the extra stuff required when writing for the web, and you're left with an inescapable, basic truth: Your web writers need to have the skill and talent to write content that's engaging, persuasive, and clear.

And that is a rare and valuable skill. Which makes it difficult to find.

It's also a challenge to engage talented writers when you're short on time and budget. Visual design isn't something everyone can do, but just about everyone's capable of stringing together words to form a sentence. It seems to make sense that you'd "leverage internal resources" to get the job done.

But the results are often less than satisfactory. As Erin Kissane (Happy Cog, AListApart.com) says bluntly, **"Web copy is still, for the most part, being written in much-less-than-ideal circumstances by people who aren't writers and don't have any time."***

Simply writing shorter paragraphs and bulleted lists for easier scan-reading isn't enough, either. Amber Simmons (AListApart.com) eloquently defends the need for better writing online:

> The distinction I make between "content" and "copy" is my own: I don't pretend this is an industry standard. But we all know copy when we read it: it's the marketing fluff that serves no purpose but to take up space. It doublespeaks and obfuscates. ... Copy is recognized by its pervasive use of agonizing words such as "leverage," "optimize," and "facilitate," or a litany of intolerable phrases such as "economically disadvantaged," "heavyset," "law enforcement officer," and "ethnic community." Writing like this is self-conscious and boring—what's wrong with saying Marvin is a poor, fat cop from the ghetto?
>
> Content, on the other hand, fills a real need: it establishes emotional connections between people. The writing has heart and spirit; it has something to say and the wherewithal to stand up and say it. Content is the stuff readers want to read.... It hooks the reader and draws him in, encouraging him to click this link or that, to venture further into a website. It delivers what it promises and delights the attentive reader.†

---

*www.alistapart.com/articles/writingcontentthatworksforaliving
†www.alistapart.com/articles/revivinganorexicwebwriting

Web writers must assume responsibility for content as being central to a successful user experience. That means being assertive about filling in the gaps between copywriting and the end user experience.

# WHEN TO CALL THE WEB WRITER

People often think of writers simply as content creation resources. But writers can have a significant impact at any part of the content lifecycle. In short, if you're looking to implement almost any part of the content strategy, you can probably ask a writer for help.

## FOR ORIGINAL CONTENT

If the web writer needs to be ready to hit the ground running during the design or development phase of a project, when is the right time to pull him into the project?

It depends. (My favorite answer.)

If the writer is working in-house for your organization, and she's very familiar with your products or services, simply give her the heads-up that the work is coming and provide her with the right tools to get the work done on time. No need to pull her in during analysis and strategic planning if you have a content strategist on board.

If, however, you will be outsourcing the work to a freelancer or agency, you may want to consider having the web writer(s) in the room at project kickoff, and possibly even during discovery workshops. Pulling in the web writer early will:

- Radically decrease the web writers, ramp-up time on the subject matter.
- Provide them with context for the larger project initiatives and overall website strategy.
- Introduce the web writers to the rest of the team early, ensuring they're recognized as valuable players in the project and not just last-minute order takers.
- Provide web writers the opportunity to ask questions and offer insights that may inform messaging, story arcs, reusable content, and so on.

Here's where I state the (hopefully) obvious: The content strategist, if time and budget allow, may in fact play the role of the web writer during design and production. I know several organizations who have in-house content strategists that are responsible not only for ongoing content analysis and planning, but also for content creation.

But sometimes, you'll need more than one web writer. Or a web writer who is supporting the content strategist. Or perhaps the content strategist is heavily focused on information architecture and content delivery (such as content modeling, CMS analysis) and may not have the specific web writing skills required for a project.

Regardless, the voice of the web writer is critical in the success of your web property (or social media campaign, or search engine results, or any kind of branded content you deliver online). **Don't marginalize the web writer's role as the person who replaces the "lorem ipsum" in your design mockups or wireframes.**

## AFTER THE SITE LAUNCHES

When you need a hand to help with site audits and content upkeep, the web writer is an obvious choice. After all, who knows your web content better than the person (or people) who wrote it in the first place?

### Neglecting your content is not an option

We've all launched something, be it a website, a campaign, whatever. Then, we usually go for drinks and celebrate. It's done! We did it! Yay.

Problem: Web content is never really finished. Sorry.

Online, once your content's out there, it's *out there*. It's live. It's A-LIVE, with a possible life of its own. People will read it, link to it, copy and paste it, blog it, call about it, and on and on. It is your audience's first impression, your first line of defense.

Don't deliver your content online and assume it will take care of itself. It won't. Put a plan in place to maintain its quality over time. For more on content maintenance, see *Chapter 11, Maintenance*. And the good news is...

### The web writer can help with content care and feeding

So, what's the web writer's responsibility in all this? Should the web writer play a part in making sure content isn't neglected or forgotten once it's live?

Absolutely. For example, the web writer can:

- Recommend revisions to current content based on web writing best practices.
- Participate in content quality checkups on a monthly or quarterly basis.
- Work with a project manager or web editor to ensure updates to time-sensitive content are delivered regularly.

The web writer can also work with a search optimization strategist to continually tweak and update metatags, links, headers, and content to ensure the content is aligned with the way people are searching for it.

There's more. A lot more. The point being this: A web writer's work is never done. And they're okay with that.

## WEB WRITING RESOURCES

Author Dan Brown (*Communicating Design: Developing Web Site Documentation for Design and Planning*) (not *The DaVinci Code*, sorry) once said, "I'm not interested in writing a book that someone else has already written."

I agree. The craft of writing for online readers has been very well explained by a few folks already. Rather than regurgitating their wise words here, I'd like to simply recommend that you pick up their books.

*Letting Go of the Words* tackles the extraordinarily important concept of content as conversation. Author Ginny Redish offers invaluable takeaways on how to craft articles, calls to action, effective help copy, and more.

*Killer Web Content* is a taut summary of the author Gerry McGovern's wildly popular web writing seminars. He delivers example after example of good versus bad. He also outlines extremely helpful metaphors you can spring on your boss to help build the case for better web content.

*Don't Make Me Think* is the classic, go-to book for understanding what makes a website usable. Author Steve Krug's chapter on web writing is worth the price of the whole book.

And thusly, herein ends my short but impassioned chapter on writing for the web... or rather, the all-important people who do it.

# 9 DELIVERY

WHEN WE THINK ABOUT how our content will be delivered online, we often jump right into which tools we can use to get it done (like a content management system).

Tools are important, but they're rarely the right place to start. It's almost like asking, "Which car should we buy?" without considering how many people you need to transport regularly (minivan or sports car?), how many miles you drive each year (fuel-efficient or SUV?), or what the weather is like in your area (convertible or 4-wheel drive?).

Don't start with the tools. Start with the content.

## THERE'S MORE TO IT THAN CHOOSING A CMS

What content needs to be delivered? When? What does it look like? How will it be created, edited, and approved? Who's going to be responsible, and for which tasks?

In this chapter, we'll answer the following questions:

- What is content delivery?
- What delivery channels are available? How do you choose the right ones for your business?
- What's the role of your CMS?
- How does social media fit in?

# WHAT IS CONTENT DELIVERY?

Content delivery is the way in which we make our content available to our audiences. Content delivery on the web is facilitated by the technical tools and media channels that get our content where we want it to be.

For our content to be truly effective, it must reach our audiences through channels that align with our business and audience goals. The mechanisms that content owners will select to deliver their content will depend not only on their target audiences' preferences, but also on time, budget, internal resources, and available tools or technologies. A content strategy can help prioritize delivery mechanisms based on a real-world analysis of all these important factors, helping move the focus from what you *can* do (because it's available) to what you *should* do (to meet your objectives).

In the context of planning our content delivery, there are three primary questions to consider:

- Who are you targeting with your content?
- Which types of content do want them to have?
- Which format do you intend to deliver?

There's another dimension to all this content delivery, as well, which is that people can take our content and republish it, mash it up with other content in other contexts, comment on it, and otherwise give it new life—good or bad—anywhere on the web. Looking at our web content through this particular lens, we may feel our content is out of our control. And it is. Which makes up-front analysis and planning that much more important: You'd better deliver the right content online the first time, because once it's out there, it's *out there.*

# WHAT DELIVERY CHANNELS ARE AVAILABLE?

To this point, we've focused primarily on content strategy as it relates to websites.

But that's just the beginning.

We deliver content via intranets. We deliver it to blogs when we comment on other people's posts. We deliver it via social media channels when we post to our Twitter account, create an event on Facebook, or upload photos to our organization's Flickr account. We send digital press releases to a variety of media outlets, which in turn publish those releases in various formats on their websites. We send email newsletters. We build landing pages. We syndicate content from other publishers and make it available on our branded web properties.

This is a book about content strategy for the web. **But really, your content strategy should inform *all* of your content which is being delivered through various channels.** It can act as a sort of command central, providing guidelines and benchmarks for all content-related efforts throughout your organization.

## NO WEBSITE IS AN ISLAND

To get content in front of our audiences, we must consider avenues beyond our website. Marketers are often assigned this task, and they have a multitude of options from which to choose:

- Email marketing
- Landing pages
- Banner ads
- Search engine marketing
- Press releases
- Video
- Mobile
- Social media

Is it possible to maintain consistency with our content messaging, accuracy, and timeliness across these different channels?

Yes. **Having a documented content strategy charges all content owners—no matter what their role or agenda—to align their communications under the same business objectives and user goals.** It also defines key messages, editorial calendars (who's doing what and when), workflows, and other important considerations for anyone delivering content to target your audiences.

## WHICH CHANNELS ARE RIGHT FOR YOUR CONTENT?

Each of these tactics offers different user experiences, targeting opportunities, messaging opportunities, conversion opportunities, and reach. But how can we differentiate between what we *can* do and what we *should* do?

### Go where your audiences are

When selecting your content delivery channels and tools, a hugely important thing to consider is *where* your audiences are—both online and off.

I'm not talking about direct mail or brochures, here. I'm talking about email, mobile, digital signage networks, video-on-demand, and other digitally-driven locations where people may access and interact with your content.

Wherever your audiences are is an opportunity to offer useful, usable information for them to interact with and respond to.

### But there's a caveat

Just because you can *find* your audiences doesn't necessarily mean it's a good place to *talk* to them. Case in point: Facebook. Brands have jumped at the opportunity to build a presence on Facebook. Some of them have been quite successful. But many of them are out of place and generally ignored. Do I really want to become a fan of my neighborhood plumber on Facebook? No. I am too busy taking the "Which Star Wars Character Are You?" quiz.

**Don't waste time delivering content where your audiences don't actually want you to be.** Get their permission. Be supportive, not interruptive. Be persuasive, not overly persistent. Meet them in the middle. (See the section later in this chapter, "Is Social Media Really All That?")

## THE ROLE OF THE CMS

Most conversations about content delivery start with the CMS. Which one should we use? (Or, which one are we stuck with?) Which features can we implement in our process? How can we structure content attributes, metadata, workflow?

Let's redirect the conversation. Please.

The role of your CMS is not simply to shuffle and store packets of information. Its primary role is to help your content strategy succeed.

## WHY DO YOU NEED A CMS?

In his book *The Content Management Bible,* Bob Boiko writes:

> The purpose of a CMS is to help organizations create and offer valuable content and functionality.

> For commercial organizations, the content and functionality aid in the sale of goods (or, perhaps, even the actual production of the goods) that are sold; for government organizations, the content and functionality aid in the running of a jurisdiction and promulgation of regulations; and for non-profit organizations, the content and functionality support a social concern.

> In each case, content supports the goals of the organization.

And, we assume, one of any organization's goals is to meet the needs of its target audiences. Which means, in turn, that the CMS must successfully deliver and manage content in ways that support the goals of the organization and its target audiences.

## YOUR KEY TO CMS SUCCESS

Your CMS success doesn't hinge on which vendor you select. You can buy the Cadillac of All CMSes, with every known feature under the sun, and the implementation can still fail. Why? **Because the tool is not the thing. The content and the people who manage it are.**

CMSMyth.com (published in partnership with ISITE Design) takes this discussion one step further:

> Many organizations now rushing to adopt web content management systems (CMS) to support their online strategies think it's the silver bullet to solve their website challenges and power content-rich applications.

But web developers, online marketers, and other front-line web pros speak of a fundamental disconnect in the promise of CMS vs. reality. Industry research and harsh anecdotal evidence indicate that 50% or more CMS projects "fail" in some way: botched implementations, soaring project costs, launch delays, ruined SEO and more.

Therein lays the central tenet of The CMS Myth: When it comes to web content management success, it's not just about the technology.

In reality, CMS success hinges on your plan, your people, and your process behind your web content management initiative.*

Read that again: Your CMS success doesn't hinge on the vendor, or features, or price point. Your CMS success hinges on your plan. Your people. Your process. Your content strategy.

## IS SOCIAL MEDIA REALLY ALL THAT?

"I want that Twitter account active tomorrow." "Let's sponsor a channel on YouTube!" "We need to get a community forum started by next quarter."

Sound familiar?

Next time someone hits you with one of these social media zingers, ask them my favorite, million-dollar question: WHY?

### ASK THE OBVIOUS

Some social media proponents tell us that the only way to protect our brand integrity in this Web 2.0 world is to "join the conversation"—get out there and pay attention to what people are saying about your products and services. Listen, respond, deliver on your promises. Be authentic. You know the drill.

But let's back up for a minute. In any conversation, we're really doing two things. We talk. And we listen. Easy enough, but here's the deal: Once you decide to actively participate in social media (like Facebook or Twitter,

---

*www.cmsmyth.com/about_the_myth.aspx

for starters), it's important that you answer two questions about your conversations:

- Why am I talking?
- Why am I listening?

These may seem like the most basic, obvious questions in the world. But they're the very first questions that must be answered before you lift a finger in social media. And it appears that many, many companies (and their agencies) are forgetting to ask them.

## THINK BEFORE YOU TWEET

So how can you use social media channels to your advantage, without losing trust or credibility? How can you mitigate risk and reap the rewards social media has to offer?

Look to your content strategy. **Plan what you're going to say, why you're going to say it, and how it's going to happen.** Don't bite off more than you can chew. Scale according to real-world resources.

Before you listen to the people who are pushing you to "dive on in" to YouTube or Facebook, you must engage marketing, PR, customer service, subject matter experts, legal. They all need to be involved in the decisions you make about social media. Because they all have important information about how your social media content and conversations could impact the business and the customer.

Sound complicated? It is. So take your time.

## IF YOU'RE GOING TO DIVE IN, DON'T
## FORGET TO KEEP SWIMMING

More than any media channel the world has ever seen, social media needs maintenance. Care and feeding. Upkeep. All. The. Time.

Before you start anything in social media, think long and hard about how much time and resources you can allocate to managing it.

Here's a screen shot of a live, sponsored YouTube channel:

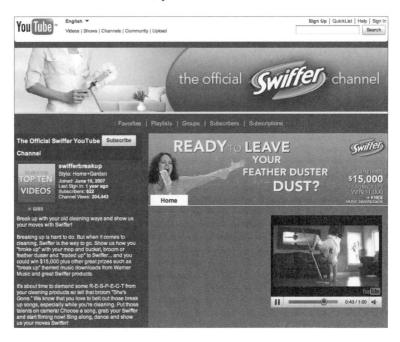

No one from Swiffer has logged onto this channel for over a year.

Clearly, there wasn't any kind of a sustainable strategy, here. At least, not one that had a meaningful outcome to either the business or its audiences.

I see this site, and I see a company that doesn't have its social media act together. And that makes me think they don't care about me, what I need, or what I have to say. Not really.

**Treat your social media efforts like a commitment, not a campaign.** Companies who truly commit to social media—who recognize that these delivery channels demand editorial oversight and regular production of branded content—are going to win the game.

# ONCE YOUR CONTENT'S OUT THE DOOR...

So you've successfully chosen the right tools to get your content to the right people, in the right place, at the right time.

Or at least, you think so.

How can you know for sure?

Assumptions won't cut it. User research and usability testing will help. But to deliver quantitative results—numbers that clearly demonstrate impact on your organization's bottom line—you'll need to measure how people are actually engaging with and motivated by your content in real time. Only then will you know for sure that your content delivery is on target.

# GOVERN

Content needs care and feeding. It needs people who are responsible for ongoing, editorial oversight. Set standards to inform changes and inspire growth. Metrics to measure its success. Useful, usable content is a process, not a product. It requires our time and attention.

# 10 MEASUREMENT

YOUR WEB CONTENT is your prospects' first impression of you, your customers' lifeline to your organization, and shapes potential employees' opinions about what it might be like to work for you.

Measure what's happening and how improvements affect content performance, and you'll win the support and funding necessary to give your audiences the content they deserve.

## MAKING THE CASE FOR CONTENT

Just asking for resources to work towards "better web content" is not going to get you anywhere with internal stakeholders. Yes, qualitative user research will demonstrate improvement (or not). If people like what you're doing, it's easy to assume that good things will follow. But a critically important part of identifying measurable results is to implement a web analytics program. Only web analytics will provide you with hard data about how content efforts have impact on your business's bottom line.

Web analytics can help you prioritize which content to focus on first. Where will your efforts have the greatest impact on your business's bottom line? How can you clean up your content to help your users find information and complete tasks as quickly and efficiently as possible? Where might additional engagement with persuasive, deeper content make a difference in your customers' life cycle?

Let's take a look at:

- What web analytics are.
- Where to begin.
- How specific methods will help inform your measurement tactics.
- Steps you can take to make incremental, measurable improvements.

*Note:* Today, measuring content effectiveness is by no means a well-defined process. In fact, it's a source of confusion and frustration to many web professionals. I'm not going to pretend to offer any set-in-stone solutions. Instead, let's take a look at where opportunities for measurement may exist in your organization.

# WHAT ARE "WEB ANALYTICS?"

Web analytics use a variety of metrics to measure user behavior online. This is an emerging discipline that's changing rapidly as technologies and methodologies evolve to capture ever-more detailed, revealing data about how customers interact with your web content.

## ANALYTICS: ASSESSING YOUR DATA

In his book *Web Analytics Demystified*, Eric T. Peterson writes:

> Web analytics is the assessment of a variety of data, including web traffic, web-based transactions, web server performance, usability studies, user submitted information, and related sources to help create a generalized understanding of the visitor experience online.

I prefer a slightly edited version of this definition. Instead of "create a generalized understanding," I'd suggest:

*To identify specific measurements and results that can inform, support, and benchmark improvements to your web properties.*

Peterson's book does a terrific job of explaining, in plain English, how to tackle web analytics, how to implement a measurement program, and how to execute a "continuous improvement process" based on your results. There are literally dozens of metrics you can track and combine for endless data streams about an infinite number of online touch points with your users.

The question is, which metrics are most meaningful to your business?

Peterson explains the different techniques and technologies used in web analytics, including:

- Web traffic data.
- Web transactional data.
- Web server performance data.
- Usability studies.
- User-submitted information and related sources.
- Forms-based data.

If you're not sure where to start, consider engaging a web analytics consultant to weigh in.

## GET CLEAR ABOUT WHAT YOU WANT TO MEASURE

When people call me and ask for my help with their web content, one of the first things I always ask is, "What do you expect to achieve with these efforts, both for your business and for your customers?"

**Before you're able to measure the effect of improvements to your web content and related internal processes, you must define measurable objectives for what you want these improvements to achieve.** These objectives should be specific and directly tied to your larger business strategy, which assumedly includes continuous improvement in customer conversion and retention.

Peterson recommends establishing baseline metrics to measure:

- Reach
- Acquisition
- Conversion
- Retention

It's important to tie these metrics to the two key drivers of your content strategy: business objectives and user goals.

## BUSINESS OBJECTIVES

Your measurable business objectives for your web content should be specifically informed by your organization's overall web and business strategies.

When it comes to web content, connecting our organization's business objectives from our own day-to-day agendas may be a challenge for some people in the workplace. Sometimes, the things we are individually asked to accomplish—and for which our performance is judged—may not seem to have impact on the "bigger picture" of our web content. Marketers are asked to drive conversion rates. Usability experts are asked to improve customer experience feedback. Content managers are asked to cut production costs. These performance metrics may seem to conflict more than they encourage collaboration.

Start with what you know, from as high up the food chain as possible. Is this year's organizational focus on growth? Stability? Internal process improvement? Innovation? Diversification? All of the above?

Next, is there a larger web strategy that's clearly informed by business objectives? What are the measurable objectives defined within it? How might these objectives be met—wholly or partially—by improvements to content and content-related processes?

Your content strategy is well-informed by these objectives. **Push to assign hard numbers to outcomes clearly tied to your content and process improvement efforts.** These are your success metrics against which you'll measure all changes in user activity and feedback.

## CUSTOMER AND USER GOALS

Gerry McGovern, the author of *Killer Web Content,* strongly advocates identifying your customers' "top tasks"—the actions people most want to take online—and using those findings to drive all improvements for both web content and transactions.

**Discovering how your users behave on your site is one of the key findings that can help prioritize changes and help you understand where to focus your content improvement efforts.**

Examples of user goals when they arrive at your website might be:

- Comparing multiple products and purchasing with confidence.
- Finding information that will help them complete a specific task.
- Reading what other customers have to say about your products and services to inform a decision about whether to do business with you.

- Contacting customer service.
- Learning about how changes to your products or services will have impact on them, personally.
- Making changes to their customer profiles or accounts.
- Applying for a job.

When making decisions about how you'd like to see related metrics improved, again, be sure to assign specific numbers (such as "Returning visitors will increase by 15 percent" instead of "Significantly increase the number of returning visitors") to your goals.

## KNOW WHERE YOU ARE NOW

Before you implement any kind of a program to manage your content strategy efforts, it's important to get as much information as you can about what's currently happening with your web content, and how content improvements might have impact on your bottom line.

It's likely you have some metrics or findings available to you now. Consider which ones may best inform future investments in improvements to your web content. If you aren't sure where to begin with analysis and implementation, work with an experienced analytics consultant or vendor. They should be able to help you decide which metrics mix will best inform and prioritize your future web and content strategy efforts.

The most important thing here is to document, document, document. **Make sure you have clearly defined data points about what you know, how you know it, where you'd like to see change occur, and by how much.** Getting that information in front of your stakeholders *before* you undertake any content or process improvements will ensure you have the necessary data to measure changes that you can directly link to your content improvement efforts.

## MEASURE CHANGE OVER TIME

If you work for an organization that's constantly demanding "quick wins," a full-scale content strategy may be a very difficult sell. Improving content and content-related processes takes time; changes to customer engagement and response may take even more time to realize.

Try to set expectations that measuring changes to key performance indicators is necessary to get a full picture of how future content improvements actually affect those KPIs. People take time to discover and adjust to new content; employees take time to adopt new processes; incremental improvements may win incremental changes that—when considered as a whole—make a larger difference.

Another important reason to measure over time is to make sure that you take into account the ebbs and flows of any web site. You don't measure a retail site only during a holiday, for example, because you'll get skewed results.

Regardless, be clear about how you plan to schedule and track your web analytics over time. Communicate your intentions, and figure out how you'll keep people informed along the way.

## PUT IT ALL TOGETHER

To my knowledge, some of the most exciting work in content effectiveness measurement is being done by a London agency called Content Delivery and Analysis (CDA).

One of CDA's partners and founders, Clare O'Brien, contributed this comment to the 2009 Content Strategy Google Group:

> [To measure content effectiveness], we have to be able to fix hard measures to what is otherwise a soft target.

> To begin, we need to understand what people will find useful. Call it a benchmark. Then, we need a framework that lets us "plan" (and audit) content in line with this benchmark. That same benchmark will also let us select which metrics we need to use to track whether the content plan is working (traffic figures, purchase/sign-up rates, pass-on rates, number of pages, etc.—they'll change with every project). These are engagement indicators.

> Then, we need to be able to check back with the most important constituent and find out what our users really think. This has to be a continual process. Ultimately, it must contribute to a quantitative output that rapidly shows us (for instance) what's right, what's flawed, what's damaging, and—critically—why.

CDA has developed something called the Content Usefulness Toolkit (CUT). Here's how they see analytics, user research, content audits, and customer insights all working together to deliver solid measurement opportunities for content effectiveness.

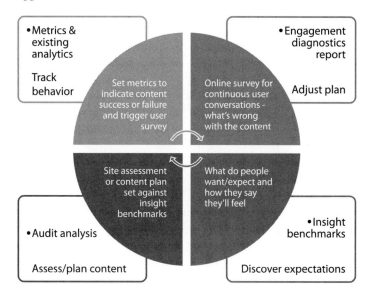

CUT Score Copyright Content Delivery & Analysis LTD 2008-9

We're used to thinking of new design and structure as the primary drivers for behavioral change. However, if we can begin to shift our focus to content—to consider how content causes significant shifts in user perceptions, behavior, and expectations—I believe we'll start seeing more breakthrough measurement methodologies that allow us to clearly ascertain content value and effectiveness.

## MEASUREMENT DRIVES CHANGE.

Measuring the impact of your content strategy against your organization's KPIs is the only way you'll ever build a business case for continual, ever-increasing investment in your web content.

Don't bother trying to tell your colleagues they should fix the content because "it's the right thing to do." Show them.

# 11 MAINTENANCE

YOUR WEB CONTENT will never take care of itself.

Once you deliver content anywhere online, particularly on your website, it's critically important that you maintain the content over time for accuracy, consistency, timeliness, and relevance to your audiences.

In other words, stop thinking "launch." Start thinking "lifecycle."

## THE LONG-TERM SUCCESS OF YOUR SITE DEPENDS ON MAINTENANCE

Web content quality—and, ultimately, your business results and user satisfaction—benefits tremendously from ongoing "health and wellness" checkups: regularly-scheduled qualitative audits that provide the opportunity to add, improve, fix, or remove content.

Caring for your content requires a well-designed process that continues over time. In this chapter, we'll look at the key points to designing a maintenance process. We'll discuss:

- What kind of maintenance your content needs.
- How to set rules for content updates.
- Who is going to take care of your content.

# WHY DO YOU NEED A MAINTENANCE PLAN?

As an important part of content strategy, a content maintenance plan outlines specific recommendations to keep web content accurate, on-brand, and on-message. It documents which content elements require editorial oversight and upkeep, as well as when each should be updated or changed. It also details who's responsible for the content, when activities should occur, and which guidelines must be followed when updating or removing content.

Don't let old, useless content clog your site search engines. Don't let inaccurate content creep its way into web search results. Dedicate the necessary time and resources to take care of your content. And plan for it up front so you're sure it's achievable.

## PLAN OBJECTIVES

There are several objectives your maintenance plan may work to achieve. Examples may include:

- Ensuring accuracy and consistency of information.
- Confirming page links, menu items, and other navigational elements are in working order.
- Maintaining integrity of brand voice and tone.
- Updating metadata to conform to new web or site search standards.
- Archiving or reorganizing older content.
- Removing redundant or outdated content.

## WHAT YOUR PLAN INCLUDES

Documenting which content requires what kind of updates and oversight is absolutely necessary if you're going to ensure that your content remains relevant and valuable to your audiences.

In addition to which content requires oversight and updates, a content maintenance plan outlines:

- Tasks involved in maintaining content.
- Estimates for how long each task should take.
- Roles required to complete all tasks.
- General skill sets required for each role.

# WHICH RULES SHOULD BE FOLLOWED?

The practice of establishing policies, standards, and guidelines provides an opportunity to bring together (often competing) web stakeholders in a forum where disparate needs and production practices can be aired, aligned, and replaced by set parameters.

This opportunity is hugely important when planning and executing a content strategy. As we've discussed, content is a complex, political, emotional topic for many stakeholders, for many reasons. **Having enforceable, well-documented rules for the web makes a huge difference in any web project process.**

WelchmanPierpoint is a consulting firm that specializes in web operations management. The following paragraphs draw upon the blog post "Web Strategy: A Definition," by founding partner Lisa Welchman, who defines what web policies, standards, and guidelines are, and how they benefit an organization.*

**Web policy** refers to a set of legal, compliance-related, editorial and technical constraints for web development. These constraints are mandatory for all web contributors. Policies work to protect the organization from risk, ensure that the organization is in compliance with any regulatory concerns, and otherwise operating within the bounds of the law and good practices.

**Web standards** provide explicit parameters, limits, and exceptions to be used by all web contributors. They should cover design and editorial; information organization and access; web tools and applications; and network and server infrastructure concerns. Web standards help raise consistency and quality, which contribute to a better user experience. They also reduce the opportunity for conflicting editorial, structural, or technical approaches to web development.

**Web guidelines** are a generally understood set of best or good practices that those contributing to the organizational web presence ought to follow. It allows the organization to express an approach to creating content, tools, and applications—as well to adopting new technologies and practices—without constraining creativity.

---

* www.welchmanpierpoint.com/blog/web-strategy-definition (edited and adapted with permission)

**For content creators, reviewers, and approvers, it's necessary that there are set rules for content that everyone can refer to and agree upon.** Otherwise, everything is always open to personal opinion, which will end up making your review process sort of like trying to tame the wild west.

When going through various stages of content review, you'll consider things like voice, tone, information accuracy, relevance to each audience, timeliness, and so on. Each reviewer may be invested specifically in one of these areas of focus, which is fine. But when it comes to specific policies and standards, everyone needs to be up to speed.

# WHO'S GOING TO TAKE CARE OF YOUR CONTENT?

In some cases, the content strategy may outline job descriptions for the individual or team responsible for content maintenance.

These roles often include the following responsibilities.

## WEB EDITOR-IN-CHIEF

A web editor-in-chief is tasked with helping to establish and enforce all web content policies, standards, and guidelines. Depending on the scale of web properties and initiatives, the editor-in-chief may serve either as an executive function—largely to oversee teams of web editors, and to facilitate their interaction with other business units and web contributors—or as a functional editor, who works directly with web writers to ensure content quality and accuracy.

This is the person who is ultimately responsible for setting and communicating standards that will shape your web content, whether on your corporate website, your intranet, in social media, or anywhere else your company distributes content on the web.

The EIC is responsible for the education and professional growth of creators. He may also take the lead on educating requesters, providers, and reviewers/approvers on what your web content standards and processes are, and how they can expect to engage with creators and publishers.

The EIC absolutely must be a lead player in any content strategy initiative. No one will be closer to your organization's web content, and no one will be more deeply invested in its constant improvement.

Finally, if anyone is going to be familiar with the day-to-day challenges of dealing with web content, it will be your EIC. This person should weigh in on decisions like resource planning and management, content management technology purchases, and other operational considerations.

A web editor-in-chief:

- Sets and communicates web content standards.
- Motivates and develops the staff.
- Participates in web strategic planning.
- Participates in web operational planning.
- Is empowered to say "no."

## WEB EDITOR

Web editors plan and oversee the ongoing management of a website and the publication of content to it. This may involve writing original copy, or coordinating and editing contributions from others. The web editor also will maintain the web editorial calendar and maintenance plan. Although the role is usually mostly journalistic, it may also require technical skills and strategic planning abilities.

This role is necessary to maintain content quality, consistency, and relevance on your website. The web editor functions as gatekeeper to ensure new content is consistent with site strategy and relevant to users. The larger your website, the more web editors you will likely need.

A web manager or editor:

- Sets guidelines for the editorial tone, style, and voice of all content.
- Establishes a style guide and editorial procedures.
- Oversees the development of all content.
- Develops and oversees the web editorial calendar and maintenance plan.

## WEB WRITER

The web writer is responsible for producing accurate, compelling copy that clearly conveys the required messages to the target audience. She must write in an appropriate style that is in keeping with your organization's brand and that supports your web content strategy objectives.

She may also need to specify where additional assets, such as images or diagrams, sound or video should accompany the text, and provide appropriate captions for them. In addition, it is the writer's job to indicate any hyperlinks within the text, and to specify clearly where they should lead.

The writer may also be responsible for providing metadata, such as keywords and a short description, to accompany each web page.

The web writer:

- Develops all required web copy.
- Works to enhance, edit, and reformat legacy and newly-created web copy to conform to web writing best practices.
- Ensures all content conforms to your web SEO requirements and best practices.

## SEARCH ENGINE OPTIMIZATION STRATEGIST

An SEO specialist analyzes your website's business objectives, content, and intended audiences in order figure out which SEO strategies will win prominent listings in the results pages of web search engines.

This person should collaborate closely with web editors and writers to ensure keywords and phrases are incorporated into the site content. She should also be in touch with your development team to ensure technical implementation of web pages or content modules isn't interfering with SEO efforts.

SEO techniques change frequently, so a large part of the SEO specialist's job involves research, self-study, and reading in order to stay abreast of developments.

## REVIEWERS AND APPROVERS

Reviewers and approvers include subject matter experts, product or service managers, legal counsel, and other key stakeholders who are able to provide insight and information for the website. These individuals are typically "wrangled" by either the web editor or content strategist during the web content development process.

It's very important to give reviewers and approvers a timely heads-up about when they'll be required to spend time with content drafts. It's all too common to turn over content with a request for review or approval by a certain date, only to have that date come and go without a response. Remember that web content is not a day-to-day responsibility for these folks, and it's likely to fall at the bottom of their to-do lists. By engaging them early and setting clear expectations about what you'll need from them, you're more likely to get it when the time comes.

## WHEN WILL MAINTENANCE HAPPEN?

There are two things to consider when documenting the answers to this question: your content workflow, and your established editorial calendar.

**A content workflow** is discussed in detail in *Chapter 7, Workflow*. It's essential to planning when your content maintenance will happen.

**An editorial calendar** identifies when and why content will be updated. Triggers may include new product or service launches, holidays, marketing campaigns, and so on.

Maintenance may also occur as part of an ongoing content quality program. Mark McCormick, Vice President of Customer Experience at Wells Fargo, compares ongoing content quality assurance with painting the Golden Gate Bridge: "You start at the beginning and, over time, slowly work your way across the entire bridge. And then you start all over again. And again. And again."

## WHEN CAN YOU STOP WORRYING ABOUT YOUR CONTENT?

When content is removed—archived or literally deleted—from your website. The end.

# 12 PARADIGM

IF YOU'VE MADE IT THIS FAR, you must think there's something to this content strategy thing. And that pretty much makes me ecstatic.

Now, here's what's next.

You're going to have to do some work to convince people this thing is worth doing. You'll need to document business cases. Deliver content audits that shine the light on your current content crises. Call out established content processes (or lack thereof) that are contributing to a mediocre end product. And you need to do all this work before anyone will even *begin* to consider your ideas.

But even after you do all that, I can't promise you that content strategy will be the silver bullet you've all been waiting for. For many of us, to introduce content strategy into an organization whose leadership views content as a commodity and the web as "just a channel" may very well be a losing battle.

Of course, fighting that battle may also be the important contribution you can make to elevating your organization's web presence from "good enough" to great.

## IF YOU'RE GOING TO WIN ONLINE, YOU HAVE TO CHANGE YOUR GAME

Just as a home page redesign rarely solves your website's larger problems, a one-time content audit or half-baked editorial calendar isn't going to fix what's wrong with your content. If you're going to commit to content strategy over the long-term, you'll need to work with leadership and other web strategists to accomplish the following things:

- Push "user experience design" off the pedestal.
- Get a real web strategy.
- Recognize content as a valuable business asset.
- Empower the content strategist.

There are organizations who have succeeded in creating a wholly new paradigm for the way they manage their content. I believe yours can, too. But you may have to focus early efforts on changing the way your coworkers see the web.

# PUSH "USER EXPERIENCE DESIGN" OFF THE PEDESTAL

Online, people search. Browse. Read. Engage. React. Transact.

These activities (and more) make up what's commonly referred to as the "user experience." And thousands of web professionals have committed their careers to designing that experience.

The core theory of UX design is this: If we craft online experiences that delight our users, our businesses will be better positioned to succeed on the web. And I agree wholeheartedly with this idea. What I don't agree with is the way in which the majority of people who call themselves UX designers deal with content.

That is to say, they don't.

## A PICTURE'S WORTH A THOUSAND WORDS (OR THE LACK THEREOF)

Although it's nearly ten years old, *The Elements of User Experience* by Jesse James Garrett is still a highly relevant book for organizations struggling to understand how people behave online. When it was first written, the book had a significant—and generally positive—impact on the way people approached web projects. It put the focus of our businesses' online efforts exactly where it belongs: on our users and their needs. Its dramatic influence on our industry continues to manifest in the way agencies and organizations plan, staff, and execute web initiatives today.

Nearly ten years later, everywhere I go, Garrett's *Elements of User Experience* diagram is still hung in cubicles, handed to me at meetings, or referred to in the context of the online customer experience. Here's what it looks like:

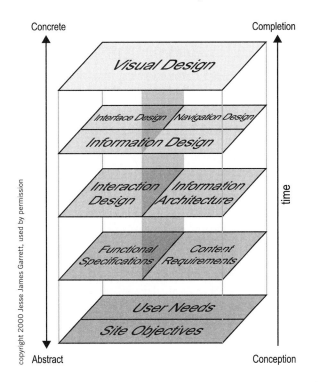

Note that content shows up in what people assume is "phase two" of the UX design process. It's referred to as "content requirements," and it appears to happen at the same time functional specifications are gathered and defined.

What this implies is that content needs can be tackled as requirements, the way we approach functional specifications and business requirements. But when we're defining functions, what we're in fact defining are *features*. And folks, if we've learned anything at all, it's that **content is not a feature**. It's a complex, ever-evolving, intricate body of information that requires ongoing care and feeding. It's not something you can check off on a list and be done with.

Although that's exactly what this diagram suggests. After level two, content disappears altogether.

Garrett is the first to say that he never intended this diagram to define the web development process. If that were the case, I wish he'd skipped the little arrow at right that shows "time" from concept to completion. Because, everywhere I go, this is exactly how web projects are run.

## UX DESIGNERS DON'T HAVE *TIME* FOR CONTENT

In a 2007 UXMatters.com article titled "The Five Competencies of User Experience Design," Steve Psomas identified the following five competencies as core to the UX designer skill set. His viewpoints are a fairly accurate representation of how user experience design is typically discussed among web professionals, so they're worth examining in this context:

- **Information architecture.** "The IA is responsible for designing a user interface (UI) structure that satisfies the corporate business strategy, product strategy, and user experience strategy and accommodates all use cases and product requirements."

- **Interaction design.** "The interaction designer bears the greatest load and is responsible for conceptual design, [diving] deepest into the minutia of page elements, presentation, and page flow."

- **Usability engineering.** "[The usability engineer] studies the discrepancies between expected and actual user behavior… conducting usability test sessions, evaluating the findings of a usability test, and making design recommendations."

- **Visual design.** "Visual design communicates your brand…. But it also communicates interactivity, information structures, workflows, and relationships between the elements and components on a screen, making it an essential aspect of UX design for applications—whether for the desktop, the Web, or mobile devices."

- **Prototype engineering.** "Ideally, an interaction designer and prototype engineer work closely together to deliver prototypes of concept models for testing by the usability engineer."*

Where. Is. The. Content?!

One has to assume most UX designers are so busy keeping up with these five "core competencies" that they just can't be bothered with the content. And that's a shame, because it's poor quality content that often damages the user experience beyond repair.

## UX DESIGN ISN'T THE ANSWER.
## COLLABORATION ACROSS DISCIPLINES IS.

To be frank, I'm of the belief that "user experience design" isn't actually a viable practice. I think it's really an umbrella term for several related but separate practices, all of which are at least somewhat interdependent with content strategy.

If you take content strategy out of the mix, you marginalize one of the key components of a successful user experience: the content. So we need to stop talking about user experience design as though it were the end-all, be-all of web professions. Instead, we need to start talking about how we can take responsibility, together, to get the job done right. *All* of it.

# GET A REAL WEB STRATEGY

While the content strategist may successfully align stakeholders from project to project on approach and objectives, without a governing web strategy, the strategist has to start from square one every time a project kicks off again.

"Web strategy" is another one of those terms that's constantly thrown around by organizations and agencies. It means a million different things to a million different people. I, myself, have committed to Lisa Welchman's definition of web strategy. It's not sexy. It's not easy. But I believe her version of web strategy is essential for organizations to sustain a successful, meaningful online presence over the long term.

---

* www.uxmatters.com/mt/archives/2007/11/the-five-competencies-of-user-experience-design.php

**Welchman defines web strategy as "the translation of organizational objectives and values into high-level management directives for the web."** She identifies two primary activities necessary for establishing a web strategy:

- Establishing a set of guiding principles for the organization's web presence.

- Formalizing a structure of authority for the web in the organization.

Welchman calls for web strategy to be "the 'first cause' for a high-quality, mission-centered, low-risk organizational web presence." It establishes formal policies for web governance, creates a framework for a web execution division, and establishes enterprise-wide measurement tactics. The result is that everyone in your organization has benchmarks that inform all online efforts to ensure strategies and tactics are in clear alignment with your organizational mission.

In one of his always helpful and insightful emails to me, Jeff MacIntyre (Predicate, LLC) pointed out that content strategy backs into organizational web strategy all the time:

> Content strategy veers right into the operational life of organizations. It's not an annual checkup, not a periodic redesign, not an organizational intervention. In fact, content strategy scales, fairly seamlessly, from the strategic layer to the everyday regimen of how your data is structured, published, and delivered.*

Content strategy can manage scope, cut unnecessary costs, and radically improve your content quality. It can ensure your content efforts are supporting larger business objectives and established user goals.

But for all this to be truly achievable and sustainable over time, your content strategy practice has to exist within a larger, established organizational web strategy framework.

---

*The quoted paragraph is from an email by Jeff MacIntyre to Kristina Halvorson.

# RECOGNIZE CONTENT AS A VALUABLE BUSINESS ASSET

When you value web content as a business asset—rather than marginalizing it as a commodity, project, or necessary evil—you have a responsibility to care for it as such. And when you put the processes in place to do so, you're well on your way to building a meaningful, sustainable online presence that will likely have a noticeable impact on your bottom line.

If you're reading this book, I'll assume that your web presence is central, or at least has impact on, to people's perceptions of your company. Based on the online experience you deliver (or don't), people will form lasting impressions of your brand, your service offerings, and your commitment to customer care. And content, as we've discussed, can make or break your users' online experience.

## IT CAN BE DONE

Need proof of concept? Here are a few examples of companies who treat web content as a business asset that drives their success online:

- Wells Fargo has a staff of content strategists who are tasked with participating (or at least weighing in) on all organizational web projects. As one of their many activities, the content strategy team also drives a "content effectiveness program" that requires ongoing content assessments across Wells Fargo's entire web presence.

- IBM.com has an Editor-In-Chief who is responsible for setting content standards, participating in multiple web content governance boards, initiating and overseeing content improvement programs, and creating and communicating governance standards to a very large staff of web content professionals.

- REI (an outdoor sporting goods and lifestyle retailer) has a staff of content strategists, editors, and writers who contribute regularly to the "Expert Advice" section of their website, which includes articles and videos offering education about how to enjoy the great outdoors.

- Mint.com (an online personal finance service) is one of the best examples I've found of a website that's clearly dedicated to superior content. Its brand is brought to life with content that's written with a

conversational tone and a focus on the customer (that is, it's all about *you,* not all about *us*). Their investment in content as a key driver to online success has, in my opinion, contributed directly to its current standing as the country's leading online personal financial service.

## YOU—YES, *YOU*—MUST BUILD THE BUSINESS CASE.

There is no one better positioned to sell the need for content strategy into your organization than you are. You have the ability to gather information—numbers, business objectives, process challenges, content audits—that, when presented as a whole, can demonstrate the need for (and potential return on!) content strategy.

At the time of this writing, I'm not aware of a single case study available to the public that documents a content strategy success story. This, of course, is a problem. If there were a Forrester report that provided charts and data and Venn diagrams about how content strategy has demonstrated mea-surable ROI (return on investment) in dozens of organizations, we'd all have a much easier time selling content strategy into our companies. But there's not.

That leaves you to figure out how and when to present your case. And remember, just because better content is "the right thing to do" doesn't cut it. **You need to clearly identify ways in which content process and quality improvements will support business objectives and, hopefully, have impact on the bottom line.**

A business asset is something that is of value of a company. Your web con-tent can be an asset, but you'll need to explain how and why before you can expect to gain stakeholder buy-in and support.

# EMPOWER THE CONTENT STRATEGIST

A content strategist is, by definition, fully invested in helping to actualize the dream of better content and improved content processes.

This person will investigate and collaborate. Analyze and synthesize. Mediate and remediate. (If you're lucky, they'll also have mad rhyming skillz.)

If you give the content strategist the support and authority to dig deeply into your web content and the ecosystems in which it lives, you will get answers to questions you didn't even know you had. You'll be presented with recommendations and solutions that will improve your content quality, deliver on your online users' expectations, and support your core business objectives.

If you force the content strategist into a narrowly defined role that essentially relegates him to a life of order-taking and production, you will never realize an iota of the benefits content strategy can offer.

Every content strategist I've ever met is passionate about content. It's part of what leads people to the job. They have backgrounds in library sciences, journalism, information architecture, copywriting, technical writing, and any other profession that deals with content as its primary currency.

Give them the tools and support they need to succeed, and content strategists will deliver for your business in spades.

# NOW, GET TO WORK!

Congratulations. You've officially made it through *Content Strategy for the Web*. And that means you're ready to hit the ground running.

As an informed advocate for content strategy, it's now *your* job to get out there and figure out what else can be done to improve the way we plan, create, deliver, and govern our web content.

Dig into the details. Defend your position. Reach out to the growing content strategy community. Exchange ideas. Share experiences. Demand better content. There's serious work to be done. And when it comes to content strategy, my friend, it's up to *you* to change the game.

So, get busy. There's a whole lot of content that needs your help. Go on out there and dig in. Be brave. Be informed. Be awesome. Be a passionate advocate for content strategy.

## CONTENT STRATEGY READING LIST

*Building Findable Websites: Web Standards, SEO and Beyond*
by Aarron Walter

*Communicating Design: Developing Web Site Documentation for Design and Planning*
by Dan Brown

*Content Management Bible*
by Bob Boiko

*Don't Make Me Think*
by Steve Krug

*The Elements of User Experience*
by Jesse James Garrett

*Information Architecture for the World Wide Web*
by Peter Morville & Louis Rosenfeld

*Killer Web Content: Make the Sale, Deliver the Service, Build the Brand*
by Gerry McGovern

*Letting Go of the Words*
by Ginny Redish

*Managing Enterprise Content: A Unified Content Strategy*
by Ann Rockley

*The Necessary Art of Persuasion*
by Jay A. Conger

*The Paradox of Choice: Why More Is Less*
by Barry Schwartz

*Web Analytics Demystified*
by Eric Peterson

*The Web Content Strategist's Bible: A Complete Guide to a New and Lucrative Career for Writers of All Kinds*
by Richard Sheffield

# ABOUT THE AUTHOR

**Kristina Halvorson** is the founder and president of Brain Traffic, a nationally-renowned agency specializing in content strategy and web writing. She is recognized as one of the world's leading content strategists.

Kristina has helped raise the international profile of content strategy as an emerging discipline that's essential to delivering useful, usable content online. Her article, "The Discipline of Content Strategy" (*A List Apart, Issue 274*, December 2008), helped introduce and define the practice to a global audience. In 2009, she co-curated the first Content Strategy Consortium to facilitate a national dialogue about content strategy and its role in the web design and development industries. She has appeared as a featured speaker at Web 2.0 Expo, IA Summit, Future of Web Apps, An Event Apart, Voices That Matter, Online Marketing Summit, SXSW Interactive, Usability Professionals Association, and j. boye.

Since 1997, Kristina has led hundreds of content projects for a diverse range of clients across dozens of industries. She is a past president of the Minnesota Interactive Marketing Association (MIMA), one of the country's largest and most active IMAs. Her professional background includes copywriting, marketing, sales, public relations, and playwriting.

When she's not traveling the country making the case for better web content, Kristina can be found hanging out at the Brain Traffic offices in Minneapolis, or at home in St. Paul with her husband John and their two lovely children.

## ABOUT THE TECHNICAL EDITOR

**Melissa Rach** is director of content strategy at Brain Traffic, a leading content strategy and web writing agency. She developed Brain Traffic's content strategy process and core tools, and leads a team that tackles messy content problems for Brain Traffic's clients every day.

Rach began working on online projects as a journalist in 1993. Since then, she's become a respected authority on how organizations use interactive content to communicate effectively with their target audiences. Providing a unique combination of skills in information architecture, messaging, writing, and communication planning, she has consulted for a wide variety of clients including General Mills, Best Buy, Target, United Health Group, Wolters Kluwer, and Wells Fargo.

Rach's methodologies have been taught at universities nationwide and recognized in books for nearly a decade. Throughout *Content Strategy for the Web* you'll find Rach's insights—from the overall content strategy process to specific messaging and content organization techniques.

Melissa lives in Minneapolis with her husband, daughter, and ginormous dog. She has degrees in journalism and archaeology from the University of Wisconsin. She'd like to thank Kristina for the opportunity to help on this book—and for inspiring a new generation of content professionals.

# INDEX